USE THE ORDER FORM BELOW TO ORDER ADDITIONAL COPIES OF

WHERE SHALL WE LIVE?

As long as the publisher's stock permits, additional copies of WHERE SHALL WE LIVE? may be ordered at the following prices:

	Price per copy
1 to 4 copies	$1.50
5 to 9 copies	$1.25
10 to 49 copies	$1.00
50 or more copies	$0.75

ORDER FORM

To: Sales Department

University of California Press
Berkeley 4, California

Please send me .... cop... of WHERE SHALL WE LIVE?

I enclose a check/money order in full payment.

NAME ....

ADDRESS ....

CITY .... ZONE ...... STATE ....

Please print or type name and address.

Payment in full must accompany order. Please do not send cash or postage stamps.

Residents of California add 4% sales tax.

WHERE SHALL WE LIVE?

WHERE
SHALL
WE
LIVE?

Report of the Commission on
Race and Housing

UNIVERSITY OF CALIFORNIA PRESS

Berkeley and Los Angeles

1958

EARL B. SCHWULST, *Chairman of the Commission*
DAVIS McENTIRE, *Research Director*
University of California Press
Berkeley and Los Angeles, California
Cambridge University Press
London, England
© *1958 by*
The Regents of the University of California
Designed by Stephen King

PREFACE

The Commission on Race and Housing is an independent, citizens' group formed in 1955 for the purpose of inquiring into problems of residence and housing involving racial and ethnic minority groups in the United States. Members of the Commission have served in their individual capacities and not as representatives of any business or other organization. As originally constituted, the Commission comprised the following seventeen members:

GORDON W. ALLPORT
Professor of Psychology, Harvard University, Cambridge, Massachusetts.

ELLIOTT V. BELL
Chairman of the Executive Committee and Director, McGraw-Hill Publishing Company; Editor and Publisher, *Business Week*, New York.

LAIRD BELL
Attorney: Bell, Boyd, Marshall and Lloyd, Chicago.

REVEREND JOHN J. CAVANAUGH, C.S.C.
Director, University of Notre Dame Foundation, Notre Dame, Indiana.

PETER GRIMM
Chairman of the Board and Director, William A. White and Sons, New York.

CHARLES S. JOHNSON
President, Fisk University, Nashville, Tennessee.

CHARLES KELLER, JR.
President, Keller Construction Corporation, New Orleans, Louisiana.

CLARK KERR
President, University of California, Berkeley.

PHILIP M. KLUTZNICK
Chairman of the Board, American Community Builders, Inc., Park Forest, Illinois.

HENRY R. LUCE
Editor-in-Chief, *Time, Life, Fortune, Architectural Forum, House & Home,* and *Sports Illustrated*, New York.

STANLEY MARCUS
  President, Neiman-Marcus, Dallas, Texas.
HAROLD C. MCCLELLAN
  President, Old Colony Paint and Chemical Company, Los Angeles.
WARD MELVILLE
  President, Melville Shoe Corporation, New York.
FRANCIS T. P. PLIMPTON
  Attorney: Debevoise, Plimpton & McLean, New York.
R. STEWART RAUCH, JR.
  President, The Philadelphia Saving Fund Society, Philadelphia.
ROBERT R. TAYLOR
  Secretary and Executive Director, Illinois Federal Savings and Loan
  Association, Chicago.
EARL B. SCHWULST, CHAIRMAN
  President and Chairman of the Board, The Bowery Savings Bank,
  New York.

Mr. McClellan resigned from the Commission following his appointment as Assistant Secretary of Commerce in 1955. Dr. Johnson and Mr. Taylor died before the Commission completed its work. To fill these vacancies the following accepted appointment to the Commission:

HENRY DREYFUSS
  Industrial Designer, South Pasadena, California, and New York.
COL. CAMPBELL C. JOHNSON
  Assistant to the Director, Selective Service System, Washington, D.C.
JOHN H. WHEELER
  President, Mechanics and Farmers Bank, Durham, North Carolina.

The Commission's inquiries extended over a period of three years, from 1955 to 1958. It has been the purpose of the Commission to conduct an impartial study comprehending all important aspects of the subject and conforming to the highest standards of scientific research. All members of the Commission accepted appointment with that understanding, and also on the basis that they would be entirely free, individually and as a body, to draw such conclusions from the study as they considered warranted.

The work of the Commission was made possible, financially, by grants from The Fund for the Republic, Inc. The Fund's participation has been limited to financial assistance, and it is not in any way otherwise responsible for the studies carried out for the Commission or for its conclusions. In the conduct of its studies and in reaching its conclusions, the Commission on Race and Housing has functioned with complete independence.

The research for the Commission was directed by Davis McEntire, Professor of Social Welfare, University of California, Berkeley. Social scientists at a dozen universities, including Atlanta, California, Chicago, Columbia, Fisk, Howard, New York, North Carolina, Pennsylvania, Texas, and Wayne, coöperated in various phases of the inquiry. Expert advice on the planning and evaluation of studies was given by the Research Advisory Committee: Stuart W. Cook, Head of the Department of Psychology, Graduate School of Arts and Science, New York University; Robert K. Merton, Chairman, Department of Sociology, Columbia University; Robert C. Weaver, Administrator, Temporary State Housing Rent Commission, New York; and Messrs. Allport, Rauch, and Schwulst of the Commission. Dr. Charles S. Johnson also served on the Research Advisory Committee until his death in November, 1956.

The focus of research undertaken for the Commission was on the problem of inequality of housing opportunity connected with minority group status, both in general and with specific reference to four groups: Negroes, Puerto Ricans, Mexican-Americans, and Orientals. Studies have examined the housing conditions of these groups, factors limiting their housing opportunities, aspects of the housing market—including the demand for housing in racially mixed areas and the effects of minority residence on property values, the social and economic consequences of racial segregation, experience with nonsegregated housing, the role of government and law, and other subjects.

In addition to information collected on a nation-wide basis, field studies have been conducted in New England, the Middle Atlantic States, the Southeast, the Southwest, the Middle West, and the Pacific Coast. Emphasis has been on the larger metropolitan areas, where housing problems involving minority groups have come most urgently to public attention.

A comprehensive report of the research findings, entitled *Residence and Race,* by Davis McEntire, is in press, scheduled to appear in 1959. Supplementary to this comprehensive report, some thirty special studies and research memoranda have been prepared for the consideration of the Commission. Some of these have been previously published or are in press; others will be published or otherwise made available for the information of those who may be interested in the specific subjects. A list of the special studies, with a brief description of each, appears as the appendix to this report.

The present report summarizes the main findings of the various studies, and the interpretations and conclusions which the Commission considers warranted by the facts. Necessarily, the discussion of many aspects of the subject is here greatly condensed. Similarly, for conciseness, documentation of sources is held to a minimum. Most of the evidence supporting the statements of fact in the present report is presented in the larger volume by the Research Director and in the reports of the several special studies.

Based upon the facts, the Commission has endeavored, in its recommendations, to suggest some feasible and sound steps toward resolving the problems centering around racial discrimination in housing.

The recommendations of the Commission and the studies upon which they are based have been made possible by the coöperation of many persons and organizations. The Commission is grateful, above all, to The Fund for the Republic for its generous financial support, extended with constant recognition of the Commission's independent status. The Research Director, his staff, and collaborators, as listed in the Appendix, have performed the basic task of collecting and analyzing the facts. Members of the Research Advisory Committee have given invaluable advice on the conduct of the research and in assessing the significance of findings.

Much of the data utilized in the inquiries for the Commission has come from governmental sources. The Commission, therefore, expresses its appreciation for coöperation extended by administrators and staffs of the United States Bureau of the Census, especially the Housing Division, the Federal housing agencies, especially their Racial Relations Services, the New York State Commission against Discrimination, and the Connecticut Commission on Civil Rights.

Other agencies that have substantially assisted the Commission's work, either by sound advice or by providing access to sources of information or both, include the National Association for the Advancement of Colored People, The National Urban League and affiliated local urban leagues throughout the country, the National Association of Intergroup Relations Officials, the Southern Regional Council, the American Friends Service Committee, the American Jewish Committee, the National Association of Home Builders, the Mortgage Bankers Association of America, the National Association of Real Estate Boards, and the National Association of Real Estate Brokers.

The studies would not have been possible without the coöperation of hundreds of local organizations, public officials, bankers, builders, realtors, and others. To all who helped, the Commission recognizes a debt of gratitude. The Commission wishes to express especially its appreciation of the contribution of its Research Director, Davis McEntire. He planned and supervised the research with exceptional competence. He combined sound scholarship with rare skill and judgment in carrying out an unusually difficult assignment.

Although drawing data from many sources and depending upon the coöperation of many people, the Commission and the Research Director have reserved to themselves all decisions, final interpretation of facts, and recommendations. Responsibility for the results, therefore, rests solely with the Commission, the Research Director, and the authors of the several studies within their respective areas. In particular, the Commission is solely responsible for the conclusions and recommendations appearing in this report.

> For the Commission
> By:
> EARL B. SCHWULST, CHAIRMAN

CONTENTS

Chapter 1

RACIAL DISCRIMINATION IN HOUSING

Exclusion and Segregation

Housing is the one commodity on the American market that Negroes and persons belonging to certain other ethnic minorities cannot purchase freely. A complex of forces and pressures operates to exclude members of these groups from residence in the majority of the nation's urban and suburban neighborhoods. The result is to segregate them in certain limited districts. In consequence, a minority person typically has fewer alternatives in housing than does a white homeseeker with comparable purchasing power. The latter may choose any location and compete for any available dwelling that suits his needs, tastes, and pocketbook, subject only to the general laws. The minority person, however, can compete freely only within circumscribed areas. Elsewhere he confronts formidable barriers because of his race, color, or ethnic attachment.

Racial restrictions on residence are an outstanding departure from the traditional American principle of freedom to move and to choose one's place of residence. Many countries do not recognize the right of free movement, but in the United States it has been so seldom challenged as to be taken for granted by most people. Exclusion from residence areas is, thus, a deprivation of a traditonal American freedom—a right legally denied only to paroled criminals, aliens, and, in the past, to certain minority racial groups.

Residential discrimination falls most heavily on people who are not white. The nonwhite population of the United States numbered nearly 18.7 million persons in 1957 according to official estimates. About 95 percent of all nonwhites are Negroes, but groups of Asian descent are an important element on the Pacific Coast and in some eastern cities. Two other groups which share many of the status disadvantages of nonwhites, including restricted

1

housing opportunity, are Mexican-Americans and Puerto Rican migrants to the mainland. The 1950 Census reported 2.3 million persons of Spanish surname in the five southwestern states, and there are probably an additional quarter of a million persons of Mexican ancestry in other parts of the country. Of Puerto Ricans there are probably not fewer than 800,000 in the continental United States at present (1958), the large majority of whom have migrated to the mainland since 1950.

Exclusion from residential areas is also directed, on occasion, against Jews. Anti-Semitic discrimination in the United States is not comparable in pervasiveness and severity to the discrimination practiced against nonwhites. Nevertheless, a recent survey, with no attempt at completeness, found housing developments barring Jews in more than a dozen metropolitan areas representing both coasts, the South, and the Middle West. The Jew has this much in common with nonwhites, Mexican-Americans, or Puerto Ricans: he cannot always be certain of a reception determined by his personal character. Jewishness, in the United States, may be less a handicap than nonwhite color or race, but it is a social handicap nevertheless and often a focus for prejudice or discrimination.

In 1957 an estimated five million persons in the United States civilian population were of Jewish faith, according to a Census Bureau survey.[1] All told, therefore, there are probably not fewer than twenty-seven million Americans, or nearly one-sixth of the national population, whose opportunities to live in neighborhoods of their choice are in some degree restricted because of their race, color, or ethnic attachment.

One of the notable social changes during recent years has been the progress of minority racial and ethnic groups toward equal status with the rest of the American people. In the past two decades, efforts to lessen racial discrimination have received a wider public hearing and achieved greater success than ever before in the history of the republic, with the possible exception of the early Reconstruction period. A series of discriminatory laws has been invalidated by the courts, which have applied with increasing rigor the constitutional guarantees of equal rights. The Su-

---

[1] An estimate of the American Jewish Committee places the Jewish population of the United States in 1957 at 5,255,000. *American Jewish Yearbook*, 1958, p. 3.

preme Court's declaration, for the field of education, that segregation is "inherently unequal" has undermined the whole system of Jim Crow legislation. At the same time, legislatures have manifested a growing readiness to enact laws against racial and religious discrimination; in 1957 Congress legislated for the protection of civil rights for the first time in more than eighty years. Discriminatory barriers have been lowered in many fields. In employment and earnings, education, military service, use of public facilities, and other areas, minority groups have gained a new status that, if not one of equality, represents measurable progress toward that goal.

Housing and residence, however, have proved probably the most resistant of all fields to demands for equal treatment. The decade 1940–1950 witnessed scant improvement in the housing conditions of nonwhites, although the white population, in spite of the general scarcity of housing, registered significant gains in housing space per capita. Segregation barriers in most cities were tighter in 1950 than ten years earlier. In the years since 1950, the exodus of whites from cities to suburbs has permitted major expansion of minority living space in cities. Housing available to minority groups has increased substantially in many cities, both in amount and in quality, but the basic pattern of exclusion and segregation has changed little, if at all. The evidence indicates, on the whole, an increasing separation of racial groups as nonwhites accumulate in the central city areas abandoned by whites and the latter continually move to new suburban subdivisions from which minorities are barred.

It is not surprising that barriers to equal housing opportunity should be among the most rigid which minority groups must face. Housing is more than physical shelter. Where a person lives bespeaks his social status, which, broadly, he shares with others who occupy the same neighborhood. The neighborhood and the house are the locale of family life and of informal, intimate social relations. To be a neighbor, therefore, is more symbolic of equal status than to be a co-worker, fellow student, or fellow organization member. But at the same time, no one can be said to be really free unless he can freely choose where he will live. The opportunity to compete for housing of one's choice is crucial to both equality and freedom. Racial discrimination in the modern world is plainly in retreat, but it will make its last stand, without doubt, in the neighborhood.

Living Conditions of Minority Groups

In no area of life are the disadvantages of minority groups more visible than in housing. In the main, these groups—Negroes, Orientals, Puerto Ricans, Mexican-Americans—occupy the slums of American cities. With the continuous flow of the white population to new suburban housing, the minorities are fast becoming the only large groups remaining in the slums.

In the larger cities, especially of the North and West, the minorities have typically lived concentrated in the oldest sections of each city, districts abandoned by previous groups, with buildings deteriorated through age and neglect. Continual migration into these areas, together with the poverty of the residents and their exclusion from other districts, has generated a chronic shortage of housing available to minority groups. This, in turn, has intensified the slum conditions through crowding and overuse of buildings. The expansion of minority living space has often taken place under conditions that rapidly spread the slum. In recent years, minority groups in many cities have gained entry to some areas of relatively good housing, but these, in many cases, are adjacent to deteriorating areas and hence are under the threat of spreading blight.

Not only have minority groups inherited slums; often new slums have been built for their occupancy. Negro districts in southern cities, Mexican-American settlements in Texas, and Negro and Mexican-American shack towns in California provide numerous examples of housing communities which have been slums from their beginning.

The visible disparity between white and minority housing conditions is confirmed by Census statistics. In 1950, more than 60 percent of all urban nonwhites and a similar proportion of urban Spanish-name households in the Southwest lived in substandard dwellings—units either dilapidated or lacking sanitary facilities. The proportion of urban white households in substandard housing was less than one-fifth. Fully half of all nonfarm dwellings occupied by Spanish-name households and a third of those occupied by nonwhites were crowded, that is, contained more persons than rooms. By the same criterion, only one in eight white-occupied nonfarm dwelling units was crowded. In dollar value, the typical nonwhite rented dwelling (nonfarm) carried a gross monthly rent of $27 as compared with $44 for white-occupied units. Nonfarm homes owned by nonwhites were valued on the average at considerably less than half the median value of white owner-occupied houses ($3,000 versus $7,700).[2]

In quality, space, and value, therefore, the homes of minority families rank far below the general standard of housing in the United States.[3] Moreover, the actual living conditions of the minority groups are generally worse than indicated by the housing statistics, because these do not reflect the environmental conditions of slum life. Slums, as numerous investigations have described them, are not merely collections of dilapidated buildings, but form a complex of unhealthful conditions: crowding of dwelling space; overcrowding of buildings on the land with resultant scarcity of parks, playgrounds, and other amenities of open space; deficient sanitation, health hazards, and fire hazards; inadequate public services; an unsavory mixture of residence with commercial and industrial land uses; and prevalence of vice, petty crime, criminals, and gangs. These conditions, with the poverty and low social status of the slum population and the profit from slum properties, reinforce each other and make it extremely difficult to effect improvements. Whether the slum dwellers make the slums or are merely their victims is an ancient question, but doubtless none will deny the extreme difficulties faced by those who wish to maintain a desirable mode of life in the midst of slum influences. For the person who desires a better life, the only practical solution is to get out, but to the person who is not of the white majority, the path of escape is often closed. Both facts are eloquently expressed in the name of a Mexican-American slum in a West Coast city: "Sal si Puedes"—"Get out if you can."

[2] Data are from the 1950 Housing Census, presented and analyzed in detail in the final and comprehensive research report to the Commission, *Residence and Race*, by Davis McEntire (in press). This basic research report is referred to hereafter only by its title.

[3] Factors contributing to the housing disadvantages of minority groups are discussed in Chapter 2 of this report.

An Old Problem in New Perspective

The concentration of minority groups in slums is not a new phenomenon, but it has acquired new significance from changing social conditions and outlooks. Many immigrant groups in the past, set apart from the general population by poverty, culture, or physical appearance, have formed compact ethnic communities, usually in the poorest housing areas of American cities. No longer replenished by large-scale immigration, these ethnic colonies have been gradually disappearing as their members become assimilated and move to nonethnic neighborhoods. Their residential areas have been taken over and expanded by the rapidly growing Negro population and also in some cities, notably New York, by Puerto Ricans. There are many neighborhoods in such cities as New York, Philadelphia, Chicago, and San Francisco which have been successively occupied by a series of minority groups.

The renewed public concern with the whole problem of racial inequality causes the housing situation and other aspects of minority status to be viewed in a different perspective than formerly. Actual living conditions of Negroes and other minority groups are certainly no worse and probably much better at present than in any earlier period, but conditions which formerly were ignored now attract wide attention.[4] In newspapers, national magazines, motion pictures, and books, the situation of the minority groups and activities seeking to overcome discriminatory barriers are constantly publicized. The American people may not yet be ready to grant full equality to minorities but obviously they wish to hear about the facts and problems.

There has developed also a new public attitude toward housing. Although the evils of bad housing have long been recognized and deplored, only in recent times have good housing for all and the elimination of slums been accepted as a responsibility of government. So long as housing was considered only a private matter, slums could be regarded as unavoidable or at least not considered a public responsibility. But when "a decent home and a suitable living environment for every American family" is declared by

---

[4] Slum housing conditions, as such, have been prominent on the agenda of social reform for many years, but public concern with the housing status of minority groups is of relatively recent origin.

Congress to be a goal of national policy,[5] existing housing inadequacies are placed in a different light. Not only is public attention focused upon the ill-housed groups, but the expectation is created that government will act or should act to help remedy the situation.

Problems of discrimination in housing have come especially to the fore in connection with public programs of slum clearance or urban renewal. Reconstruction of a slum usually requires the relocation of all or part of the resident population, either permanently or temporarily. Since the residents, more often than not, are members of minority groups, efforts to rehouse them in non-slum areas collide with segregation barriers.

Other factors magnifying the significance of racial inequality in housing are the far-reaching implications of recent and prospective population changes. The Negro population, once predominantly southern and rural, is rapidly becoming urban and national. Negro migration from the South to the North and West and from farms to cities since the onset of World War II is measured in millions. The cityward movement of Negroes has coincided with an unprecedented exodus of whites from the larger cities to the suburbs. Negroes have thus far participated only to a small extent in the suburban movement; their migrations have been overwhelmingly to the central cities of metropolitan areas, and mainly to the in-lying districts of these cities.

Because of these contrasting population movements, the Negro migration to cities has had a greater relative impact on urban population and residence patterns than would otherwise have been true. In most of the larger cities of the North and West, the white population is increasing slowly or even declining, and nonwhites have become the sole or main source of continued population growth. Puerto Rican migration to the mainland, amounting to more than half a million net since 1950, is directed, even more than the Negro, to the large cities, above all, to New York. Nonwhites (and Puerto Ricans) form a rapidly increasing proportion of the total population in many metropolitan cities, but a diminishing fraction of the suburban population. If the population movements of the past dozen years should continue unabated for a similar period in the future (which will not necessarily occur),

[5] U. S. Congress, "Declaration of National Housing Policy," *Housing Act of 1949*.

huge sections of many cities will be occupied by nonwhites and Puerto Ricans, and these groups will increase to a third or a half of the total city population. This prospect raises disquieting questions about the future of central cities as centers of business and culture.

The time-honored solution to the housing problems of immigrant minorities has been contained within the process of Americanization. As newcomers and their children learned the values and behavior of Americans and progressed economically, they moved out of the slums and found dwellings in middle-class "American" neighborhoods. In so doing, individuals ceased to be identified or to identify themselves as members of ethnic groups. Their shift of residence has been generally both a condition for, and a symbol of, upward social mobility, with emancipation from minority status. This process has been going on in American cities for at least a century. It is by no means complete but it has been accelerated by the prosperity of the postwar period and the unprecedented ease of achieving home ownership under government-insured mortgages. Among the new suburbanites is a large contingent to whom the move to a new housing tract represents not only an improvement in housing but an advance in social status as well.

The same process will probably occur with the Puerto Ricans, who are, in historical perspective, only the latest in a long series of immigrant groups. Their American citizenship and previous contacts with American culture on the Island will undoubtedly expedite their assimilation. The absence of barriers to migration, however, will allow constant replenishment of the unassimilated population for an indefinite period, although the flow of new migrants probably will be lessened by economic progress on the Island.

For groups that are not white, the traditional pathway of escape from the slums is obstructed by the color barrier. Members of these groups become assimilated culturally in the same way as others; in all that concerns ideas, values, and behavior, they may become indistinguishable from other Americans. But at the point where they are ready to enter the larger society, race discrimination bars their way and relegates them to continued minority status. The Negro population, in spite of its centuries of residence in America, has at present some of the characteristics of an incompletely assimilated immigrant group. Many Negro newcomers to cities or to the North and West or both have much to learn about northern or urban ways of living. They depend upon the segregated Negro community for social life much as the immigrant depends upon his ethnic group. Moreover, Negroes in general, and not just the new migrants, never allowed to participate fully in American society, have lagged in acquiring education, occupational skills, and behavior standards which are the means of effective participation. From slavery and restricted freedom, the lower class of Negroes has carried forward certain patterns of family life at variance with white middle-class customs. As with immigrant groups, the cultural gap between the Negro and the white populations is being narrowed as Negroes live longer in cities, gain more education, and rise in economic status. Indeed, in the past two decades their progress has been more rapid than ever before. There are now many Negroes—and their number is increasing—who have achieved middle-class status economically and culturally and are ready to move out of the segregated Negro community into the mainstream of American life. Unlike the white person of immigrant origins, they cannot do so freely. Their segregation is perpetuated and enforced by exclusion from most of the better residential areas.

Chapter 2

SUPPORTS FOR SEGREGATION

Housing Demand Factors

Many forces work to maintain the segregation of minority groups and to discourage their dispersion. Most important from the standpoint of civil rights are the pressures to exclude members of these groups from the general housing market. These pressures, exerted by government agencies, real estate brokers, builders, housing finance institutions, property owners, and others, constitute the compulsory aspect of residential segregation, but they are not, at least in the short run, the only factors supporting the actual concentrations of minority groups. In a number of reported instances, where housing opportunities have been offered outside the established minority areas, observers have been surprised to find no rush of applicants. Builders of new housing developments open to nonwhites have often commented on the thinness of the market among nonwhites for new housing, especially at a distance from existing minority communities. Developers of interracial housing projects have found that they could not take for granted a large waiting demand from nonwhites for their product. Minority communities, apparently, notwithstanding their generally unenviable living conditions, possess a considerable stability of their own, as will be shown in what follows.

Poverty is a major factor of residential stability. Because the incomes of minority families are generally low, their housing demand is mainly for the cheaper dwellings to be found most abundantly in the older and deteriorated residential areas. The economic position of the minority groups and consequently their ability to compete in the housing market have improved notably in recent years; nevertheless, the median income of nonwhite urban families is still about 40 percent lower than the median income of white families nationally, and the disparity is even greater in the South. In 1955 nonwhite families constituted about

9 percent of all American families but scarcely more than 3 percent of families with incomes of $5,000 or more per year. Obviously, a much smaller proportion of nonwhite than of white families can afford the price of good quality housing, new or used.[1] Moreover, a smaller part of the income actually received by nonwhite families, as compared to white families, is convertible into effective housing demand because of the frequent instability of income sources and the frequency of families without a male head. Builders experienced in marketing new housing to Negroes report one of their principal difficulties to be the inability of many would-be purchasers to qualify for mortgage loans according to the usual requirements.

The housing demand of nonwhites is further limited by their tendency to spend a smaller part of their resources for housing than do whites, regardless of income. Housing market analysts have commented on the apparent reluctance of many Negroes, especially in the South, to increase greatly their outlay for housing, although their incomes would permit them to do so. Statistics of the 1950 Housing Census indicate that nonwhite families tend to purchase cheaper houses or pay lower rents than do whites at each level of income. This behavior is, of course, not characteristic of all Negroes, but it is a group tendency. The reason may lie in their long habituation to poor and cheap housing or perhaps in the restricted availability of good housing to them. It may reflect a lag in the adjustment of consumer behavior to recently improved incomes. Whatever the explanation, it seems evident that nonwhites as a group compete less strongly for housing than even their limited incomes would permit.

When members of any group share a common cultural heritage or common experiences or both, it is only natural that they should seek to live in some proximity to each other. When the larger world is strange or unfriendly to members of the group, their congregating tendencies are reinforced. The group then becomes a refuge and a shield to its members. To the members of many newly arrived groups in the United States, the ethnic colony has been a place where familiar language was spoken, accustomed ways

---

[1] A detailed analysis of the economic status of nonwhites and characteristics of their demand for housing is presented in *Residence and Race*, Part II: "Minorities in the Housing Market."

of living were maintained, and where one was at home and among friends.

American Negroes, of course, are in no sense "foreigners." Few persons in the United States can claim to be more American than they. Immigrants to the United States have imported their foreign cultures and maintained them in some measure for long periods of time. The circumstances of the Negroes' involuntary coming and of their life as slaves cut them off decisively from their ancestral cultures. Negroes are not "Afro-Americans" in any cultural sense; they are wholly American. They share, however, a particular historical experience and status which has held them as a group apart from the larger society and compelled them to develop a group life of their own. Seldom accepted in white society, they must look to other members of their race for almost the whole range of associational opportunities. Negroes have developed various social institutions, above all the church, which serve them as a unifying force. Indeed, for them, perhaps even more than for other minority groups, the Negro community affords protection and release from the strain of relations with the unfriendly white world. It is the one place where the Negro can behave naturally, use freely such facilities as are available, and avoid the immediate impact of prejudice and discrimination.

All these factors of group cohesion sustain the segregation of a group by leading its members to place a value on remaining in the colony as against moving in search of better living conditions elsewhere. This observed tendency of racial and ethnic minority groups to segregate themselves is sometimes used to justify the exclusion of minority persons from other areas. Thus it is said that Negroes, for example, prefer to live by themselves or that they will not be happy in neighborhoods occupied by white people. This rationalization overlooks the fundamental fact that group self-segregation is voluntary, whereas exclusion is compulsory. It is one thing for a person to choose to live adjacent to others of his color or cultural background. It is quite a different thing to decree that he *must* live there and not elsewhere.

Just as different groups vary in the strength of their internal cohesion, so do individual members of each group differ in degree of attachment to the ethnic community. So long as an ethnic group is homogeneous and markedly different from the general population in culture or economic status, its members are likely to manifest a high degree of identification with the group, particularly if prejudice against them is severe. The long-lasting, tightly segregated Chinatowns are a case in point. Given time and opportunities, minority populations in the United States have tended to become more differentiated within themselves. As their members have entered a variety of occupations and moved upward in the scale of socio-economic position, a growing number have come to value the opportunities and goals of the larger society more than the solace of their ethnic group. This process has been accelerated in recent years by the unprecedented economic opportunities available to members of minority groups and the general lowering of discriminatory barriers. Again the Chinese afford a striking example. After two generations of immobile confinement in their ethnic slums, these people, following the last war, began an exodus which, by 1950, had substantially reduced the Chinatown populations of San Francisco and New York, notwithstanding a major increase in the total Chinese populations which occurred simultaneously.

The example of the Chinese also illustrates the importance of family structure for housing demand. Reference was made earlier to the depressing effect of the high proportion of female-headed families on the housing demand of Negroes. The Chinese, during their long period of segregated immobility, had a conspicuous absence of women and hence of families. The remarkable exodus from the Chinatowns followed the lowering of immigration barriers, which permitted the entry of thousands of Chinese women as wives of American citizens and the consequent formation of many new families.

The group cohesion or self-segregation of Negroes in cities of the North and West is currently affected by two major kinds of change. On the one hand, the number of Negroes with the incomes and cultural outlook of the middle class is increasing rapidly. At the same time, the ranks of the poor and culturally retarded Negroes are constantly replenished by migration from the South. Very different perspectives of housing characterize the two extremes. For the foreseeable future, the mass of poor and "unassimilated" Negroes will probably provide a large population for the "Negro ghetto." The growing middle class, with little in com-

mon with the lower group save color, will undoubtedly press with
rising insistence for the opportunity to live like other Americans
of their social level. A large and increasing proportion of white
Americans, apparently, is prepared to see the minorities achieve
this opportunity.

Race Attitudes and Beliefs

Underlying the exclusion of nonwhites from white neighborhoods
is the unwillingness of many white people to live in proximity to
Negroes or other minorities. Those who make decisions for exclusion usually claim to act out of respect for public sentiment.
Resistance of white to nonwhite neighbors has varied from mere
avoidance to acts of violence such as dynamiting homes acquired
by nonwhites. Not infrequently minority families have required
special police protection to occupy their homes in disputed sections of a city. Short of violence, the residents of a neighborhood
have, of course, a great many ways of discouraging a newcomer.

The race prejudice of which this behavior is a manifestation is
a complex phenomenon. To treat it adequately is beyond the
scope of the present report. Only some aspects of race prejudice
especially relevant to housing can be examined briefly.[2]

In the first place, the pressure of whites to reject nonwhite
neighbors is not universal or uniform. In virtually every large city
with a biracial or multiracial population, and in many smaller
cities as well, there are residence areas of racially mixed occupancy.
Many public housing projects and military housing communities
are open to eligible families of whatever race. In recent years, a
few private builders have successfully marketed new housing developments of a wide price range to an interracial clientele. Thus,
whatever may be said about white attitudes toward racial mingling, it is not a fact that whites always refuse to tolerate nonwhite
neighbors.

Probably the most important aspect of racial attitudes in the
United States is the conflict between attitudes on the levels of
principle and of practice, respectively. The social ideals of the
American nation, as embodied in its great political documents and

[2] This discussion is based upon research reports prepared for the Commission on
Race and Housing by Claire Selltiz and Stuart W. Cook, *Studies in the Social Psy-
chology of Race and Housing;* and Helen E. Amerman, *Studies of Attitudes Toward
Housing and Race* (see Appendix).

its religious heritage, emphasize individual liberty, equal rights, and the fundamental equality of all men. These ideals are constantly reiterated in political speeches, sermons, judicial decisions, preambles to legislative acts, and elsewhere. In flagrant contradiction of these principles are race prejudice and discrimination which deny equal opportunity to members of certain racial and ethnic groups. American principles have never required equality of men in achievement. That people should be either handicapped or favored, however, by the condition of their birth has always been repugnant to the American ethic.

Unfriendly critics often call Americans hypocritical for professing equalitarian principles while simultaneously denying equality to various groups, but probably few Americans would accept this judgment. The truth is that a genuine conflict exists between two sets of irreconcilable ideas. It is not too much to say that the race problem exists because of this conflict. If the American nation could bring itself to settle decisively the status of non-white peoples by one standard or the other, there would be less controversy. But this has never been possible. The conflict, as other observers have pointed out, is not essentially between groups of people holding opposing views, but like the struggle between good and evil, it goes on in the hearts and minds of individuals.[3]

When people hold conflicting attitudes, they are placed under the psychological necessity of reconciling or rationalizing them in some way. In the past, the principal bridge between the creed of liberty and equality and the white's will to subordinate non-whites has been the belief of the whites in the inherent racial inferiority of the darker-skinned. Modern science, however, has discredited the older theories of innate racial differences and directed attention to factors of experience and opportunity in explanation of group differences which actually exist. The spread of modern scientific views among the general population has undermined the factual basis for race prejudice and in so doing, accentuated the conflict of ideals and practice.

The trend of white attitudes toward racial questions is plainly in the direction of tolerance. This trend can be inferred from the

---

[3] Gunnar Myrdal's classic treatise, *An American Dilemma* (1942), defines the Negro problem in America as a conflict between equalitarian ideals and discriminatory practice.

growing readiness of state legislatures in the North and West to pass laws against racial discrimination. There is, in addition, direct evidence from public opinion polls. When the National Opinion Research Center, in 1942, asked a national cross section of the white population, "If a Negro family with the same income and education as you have moved into your block, would it make any difference to you?", 42 percent of the Northerners and 12 percent of the Southerners said it would *not* make any difference. The same question was repeated to a similar cross section fourteen years later, in 1956. At this date, the proportion stating no objection to residential proximity had risen to 58 percent in the North and 38 percent in the South. Replies to questions on racial integration in schools and transportation showed a similar shift. Indicative of a fundamental change in racial attitudes, both North and South, were replies in 1942 and 1956 to a question on the intelligence of Negroes: "In general, do you think Negroes are as intelligent as white people—that is, can they learn things just as well if they are given the same education and training?" The proportion of white persons interviewed who believed Negroes equally intelligent rose, in the North, from 50 percent to more than 80 percent, and in the South, from 21 percent to 60 percent.[4]

People vary widely in the intensity of prejudice toward minority groups. With allowance for shifts in the general level of prejudice and for regional differences, various studies support a conclusion that only a minor fraction of the population is strongly prejudiced. A correspondingly small fraction is strongly unprejudiced to the point of advocating racial equality. In between is the majority— probably 50 to 75 percent of the white population in cities of the North and West—who are somewhat prejudiced but who do not feel strongly about racial issues one way or the other. This large group, with no strongly fixed opinions, is capable of being influenced by education or pressures from either side.[5]

People vary also in their readiness to translate prejudiced feelings into overt discriminatory behavior. Feelings are not neces-

[4] Herbert H. Hyman and Paul B. Sheatsley, "Attitudes Toward Desegregation," *Scientific American*, 195(6): 35–39 (December, 1956).
[5] The findings of some twenty studies, carried out between 1944 and 1956, on attitudes toward mixed neighborhoods are analyzed and compared in the research reports to the Commission by Claire Selltiz and Stuart W. Cook, and Helen E. Amerman (see Appendix).

sarily acted out. Hence a person may have fairly strong racial prejudices but, for a variety of reasons, refrain from discriminatory conduct. Typical, perhaps, is the white housewife in a racially mixed neighborhood who told a social survey interviewer that she "didn't care for colored people" and was "upset" when a Negro family moved into her street. But she realized that Negroes "have to live somewhere" and did nothing to discourage the newcomers. Besides, she added, there was "nothing I could do about it, and if I said anything it would only cause unpleasantness." It is equally true that unprejudiced or slightly prejudiced persons may engage in discriminatory acts because of situational pressures. Instances are frequently reported, for example, of property owners refusing to sell their for-sale houses to nonwhites not because of personal feelings, but out of their wish not to offend the neighbors. Real estate brokers, as described below, are held in line by the policies of their boards, regardless of their personal attitudes.

Racial prejudice and discrimination do not exist in isolation but are always influenced by other factors and conditions. The operation of social institutions such as government and law often plays a major role in stimulating or weakening both prejudice and the disposition to express prejudiced feelings in discriminatory action. For example, race-restrictive housing covenants were originated by private real estate interests, but when the Federal Housing Administration put its approval on them and advocated their use, they acquired a status and a sanction which they had not had before. Some of the general factors which, in the past, have served to justify and sustain race prejudice have been discriminatory race laws in many states, certain government policies, segregation in the armed forces, and the judicial doctrine of "separate but equal." In recent years many of these supports for race prejudice have been removed. One obvious result has been to deprive race prejudice of moral sanction and social respectability. Rarely, nowadays, are sentiments of racial antagonism openly expressed in public. On the other hand, certain environmental supports for prejudice have been strengthened by recent trends. The mass migration into northern cities of hundreds of thousands of poor and culturally retarded Negroes and Puerto Ricans and the increase of social problems in the areas of their concentration have served to stimulate prejudice. In the South, public appeals to white supremacy seem to have passed out of favor, but anti-Negro hostility has drawn fresh support from identification with the traditional cause of regional independence and states' rights.

In addition to generalized racial prejudice, white resistance to minority neighbors seems to rest upon a number of rather specific fears. Some of these seem to be status anxieties, fears of property value loss and neighborhood deterioration, fear of being inundated by minorities, and fears for personal safety.

Status.—The central problem in practically all aspects of race relations is social status, and housing is no exception. The presence of minority persons in a neighborhood in the capacity of servants, caretakers, janitors, or the like rarely, if ever, attracts unfavorable notice from the whites. The latter become disturbed only when minorities come in under circumstances which imply equality of status.

Two considerations are basic: first, nonwhite color and certain ethnic origins are identified with low status in American society; second, a family shares to a large extent the status of its neighbors, and the neighborhood one lives in is a measure of his social position. Therefore, when minority people move into a neighborhood, the resident whites may feel that their own status becomes equated with that of a low-ranking group. Whites, who may themselves be relatively unprejudiced, may be sensitive to the opinion of others —their friends, relatives, or even strangers. For instance, a white woman, commenting on a Negro family's purchase of a house a few doors away, observed that it was "a fine family," the husband was a surgeon, and she had no personal objection to them whatever. But, she added, people driving by see the little boy playing on the sidewalk. "How are they to know that he is a doctor's son?"

Fears of racial intermarriage, it may be noted, are part of the status problem. Although racist ideology makes much of race purity and the evils of miscegenation, actually sex relations between whites and Negroes have provoked racial antagonism (often violent) only when the white partner was female. When whites express race-sex fears, it is practically always in relation to white women. The freedom of white men to court relations with Negro women, and the concomitant violent suppression of any Negro pretensions to white women, has always been, in the South especially, among the main symbols of white dominance. Marriage, moreover, implies an equality of status between the partners which nonmarital sex relations do not.

People vary, of course, in the extent to which they may perceive minority neighbors as a threat to their social status. The socially secure may be little concerned. But those who are striving for acceptance at a higher social level and are not sure where they stand are likely to feel threatened by the prospect of sharing their neighborhoods with members of groups to whom society attaches a stigma of low status. Thus, neighborhoods occupied by second generation ethnic groups have manifested some of the bitterest resistance to Negro entry. Many of the new suburban residents are just arriving socially on the fringes of the middle class; their anxieties about status doubtless contribute much to the determined exclusion of nonwhites from suburban housing tracts.

Property values.—In the whole field of housing and race, probably no idea is more widely or firmly held than the belief that entry of nonwhites into a neighborhood causes property values to fall. Many real estate brokers, mortgage lenders, and property appraisers hold to this belief almost as an article of faith. In addition to whatever factual validity it may have, the belief can be an excellent rationalization of prejudice because the conservation of property values is an eminently respectable purpose.

The available evidence of the effects of nonwhite entry on property values is examined in one of the special studies prepared for The Commission on Race and Housing.[6] In this report only a few salient aspects of this complex subject can be touched upon. Inquiry has found cases conforming to the common belief, but in other observed cases the movement of property values has run contrary to the popular belief. The outcome is affected by various factors other than the actual movement of nonwhites into a neighborhood.

More often than not, residential areas which nonwhites are permitted to enter are older neighborhoods where the housing is already obsolescent or deteriorating. Declining values in those districts, coinciding with nonwhite entry, have furnished much of the "evidence" for the thesis that nonwhites injure property values. In reality, values in those areas would decline in any case; the demand of incoming nonwhites for housing, replacing the loss of white

[6] Luigi Laurenti, *Property Values and Race: Studies in Seven Cities* (see Appendix).

demand, probably tends more often to support rather than depress the housing market in older neighborhoods.

Much depends on the reaction of white residents to the coming of minorities. If the whites hasten to leave, the market may be glutted by an oversupply of houses offered for sale in a short period. Then, the expectation of a fall in property values becomes a "self-fulfilling prophecy." Whites predict that values will drop with the entry of nonwhites, and when the entry occurs, they act in a manner to make the prediction realized.

On the other hand, if white residents of an area are in no hurry to leave, but nonwhites are eager to come in, the pressure of non-white demand may bid up the price of houses. Several situations of this type have been observed, with market values of property rising during a period of racial transition.

In a third type of situation, whites may not rush to leave an area but nonwhite demand may be weak, and the presence of non-whites may discourage demand from whites. In these circumstances a decline of house prices is probable. In some cases which have been studied, however, the presence of a limited number of non-whites in a good residential district or housing development seems not to have discouraged seriously white interest in the area. In-terracial neighborhoods have come into existence, with both whites and nonwhites active as both buyers and sellers, and values have remained stable.

In general, the conclusion seems warranted that nonwhite entry into residential areas does not necessarily depress real estate market values. Under certain conditions it may increase values. Among neighborhoods actually investigated for this Commission, in cities on both coasts and in midcontinent, the entry of nonwhites was found to have had either no effect or a favorable effect on property-selling prices in the majority of cases.[7] Whether entry of non-whites into a neighborhood will tend to support or depress prop-erty values, or have no effect, depends upon the housing market circumstances of the particular case. However, as a motive to ac-tion, facts are less important than what people believe to be facts; and as noted, the property-values belief, if widely acted upon, can produce its own validation.

"*Inundation.*"—The arrival or prospective arrival of nonwhite

[7] *Ibid.*

families in a neighborhood frequently generates fears that more will follow and the neighborhood will become all nonwhite. Many whites can accept the presence of a small number of minority families, but even among the relatively unprejudiced, few would be willing to live in a predominantly nonwhite district. Hence, fear of being inundated by nonwhites is often a significant motive, first, to exclusion, and second, to white evacuation of areas entered by nonwhites.

This fear has a basis of experience in the seemingly inexorable process of racial transition around the edges of existing nonwhite residential areas. Away from these areas, new all-minority communities are likely to develop only under special conditions— when they are actively promoted by commercial interests, or when various factors combine to produce exceptionally strong minority demand for housing in some particular area. In many cities there exist a considerable number of neighborhoods which have received one or a few minority families and no more.

Two principal factors conducive to racial transition in neighborhoods are the restricted supply of housing available to nonwhites and the pressure of a growing population for more living space. When a particular area is opened to nonwhites, they tend to crowd into it because of their need and lack of alternatives. However, where the supply of housing open to nonwhites is relatively adequate, tendencies to inundation of additional areas are greatly reduced.

For a neighborhood to shift from white to nonwhite occupancy, it is obvious that not only must there be a sufficient nonwhite demand, but whites must be willing to abandon the area. In many cases, areas involved in racial transition had largely ceased to be attractive to the white population even before the entry of nonwhites; nonwhite interest has provided more of an opportunity than a pressure for the resident whites to leave. As for nonwhite entry into neighborhoods still competitive in the white market, evidence indicates that whites will often remain or continue to buy into the area so long as the nonwhite proportion of the population is relatively small and does not lead to expectations that the neighborhood will become all nonwhite. If the nonwhite population increases beyond some point, the neighborhood is usually written off by the white market and tends, sometimes rapidly, sometimes slowly, to become wholly nonwhite. The turning point cannot be precisely defined but varies with different circumstances.[8]

Personal safety.—Connected with white fears of inundation is fear of being exposed to the unhealthful social conditions frequently characteristic of racial transition areas in large cities. The prevalence of juvenile crime, gang activity, and other social pathology in many areas of minority concentration is attributable to social conditions in those areas rather than to race or ethnic origin as such. The existence of undesirable social conditions is, nevertheless, a powerful motive to exodus of the remaining whites and a stimulant to race prejudice in other areas.

Housing Industry Practices

The group prejudices of the white population provide a basis and support for the segregation of minority groups, but the actual controls and sanctions are administered largely by the housing industry. It is the real estate brokers, builders, and mortgage finance institutions which translate prejudice into discriminatory action. Not all members of these large and diversified business groups discriminate against racial minorities; some are scrupulously non-discriminating and some are even crusaders for equal rights. But in the main, the services of brokers, builders, and mortgage financiers are extended to nonwhites only in limited measure and under special conditions. Spokesmen for the housing industry usually disclaim responsibility for their discriminatory practices, asserting that their actions are dictated by the prejudices of their clientele or the general public, or by the imperatives of profit and loss. There is unquestionably some basis for this defense, but it is also true that members of the housing industry often lead rather than follow the public in matters of housing discrimination. Whatever their motivations, members of the housing industry have the power to make important decisions concerning access to housing. Virtually everyone must depend in some degree upon the industry to satisfy his housing needs. The unwillingness or inability of the housing industry to make its services fully available to the members of minority groups has had the effect of creating, for those

[8] Housing market characteristics of mixed neighborhoods and interracial subdivisions are examined in several of the special studies edited by Nathan Glazer and also in the research reports by Eunice and George Grier, Luigi Laurenti, and Chester Rapkin (see Appendix).

groups, a separate housing market in which only a limited quantity and quality of merchandise is offered for sale.

Real Estate Brokers

Real estate brokers, with occasional exceptions, will negotiate the sale or rental of property to minority persons only in areas considered appropriate for minority residence, usually areas where minorities are already living.[9] To do otherwise is considered among brokers an unethical practice. Until recent years, the Code of Ethics of the National Association of Real Estate Boards contained a provision specifically enjoining realtors from being instrumental in introducing a minority person into a white neighborhood, and many local boards had similar provisions. The references to race or nationality have been removed from the National Association's Code and some ambiguous statements substituted, but from all indications the restatement has made little change in actual practice. The intent of the "ethical" provisions is, of course, to enforce uniformity of action by real estate brokers, regardless of their individual attitudes.

There is no reason to believe that real estate men are either more or less racially prejudiced, on the whole, than any other segment of the American population. However, the controls exercised by the business group over its members lead them to consistent practice of discrimination, whether or not it represents their personal choices. Real estate men are typically convinced that to "break" white neighborhoods would bring serious harm to their business. Damaging reactions are expected both from neighborhood residents and from colleagues in the real estate business. It is the latter which serves to maintain a high degree of uniformity in practice. Granted the frequently strong pressures from neighborhood residents, it is not for the individual broker to assess the situation and choose a course of action. If he desires to be considered reputable and to hold the esteem and coöperation of his associates, he must adhere to the prescribed racial practices of the real estate business. On occasion, members who violated the racial code have been expelled from real estate boards. Sanctions of this

[9] More detailed analysis and documentation are presented in *Residence and Race*, Chapter 14: "Real Estate Brokers," and the special study by Rose Helper (see Appendix).

kind are not favored, however, because they risk bringing into the open the contrast between real estate ethics and public ideals in regard to race. Other sanctions are available to hold individuals in line.

Supplementing group control of the individual, real estate brokers tend to hold in common certain theories which sustain discrimination. One of these is a belief in the social and economic virtues of the homogeneous neighborhood. For many years, real estate dealers and appraisers have been taught to value homogeneity and avoid the hazards of "incompatible groups." In the same doctrinal family are equally traditional and widely held beliefs that entry of nonwhites into a neighborhood damages property values, and that the presence of nonwhites, particularly of Negroes, places a neighborhood on an inevitable descent toward a slum. Real estate businessmen generally regard the entry of a nonwhite into a white neighborhood as an unmitigated threat to the economic and social status of the neighborhood. As an organized business group, laying stress on "ethics," realtors have assumed some responsibility to guard the racial homogeneity of white neighborhoods.

It is sometimes asserted that brokers do not initiate discrimination but only follow the wishes of their principals, the sellers, and that if the latter were willing to accept minority buyers, the brokers would be equally willing. The evidence indicates, however, that brokers generally take a more independent view of their responsibilities, and will refuse to participate in transactions which they consider improper, regardless of the wishes of individual sellers and buyers. There is no record of any real estate board's having announced that introduction of a minority buyer into a white neighborhood was permissible if the seller were willing.

Moreover, beyond the sphere of business transactions, real estate boards have occasionally taken the lead in defending racial segregation in the arena of public policy. The Los Angeles Real Estate Board, for example, urged a constitutional amendment to reverse the Supreme Court's decision against judicial enforcement of race-restrictive housing covenants. In New York City, the real estate boards led the opposition to a proposed municipal law against discrimination in private housing.

Still another way in which real estate brokers help to maintain

segregation is by expediting and guiding the process of neighborhood racial transition. When an area is likely to be entered by nonwhites, brokers usually try to hold the line against them, but only
up to a certain point. After a number of nonwhites have entered
the area, real estate agents often reverse their tactics and work to
bring in as many nonwhites as possible, while stimulating the
whites to leave. This practice is considered unethical by many
real estate boards, but the prospect of a turnover in ownership of
all the properties in a neighborhood within a short period of time
offers a tempting opportunity to real estate agents which many are
unwilling to forego. By restricting minority access to many neighborhoods and actively promoting white-to-nonwhite transfers in
other areas, the real estate brokers often exercise considerable influence on the racial pattern of residence in the direction of intensified segregation.

A further aspect of the race relations of the real estate business
that merits notice is the exclusion of nonwhite real estate brokers
from the professional associations of real estate men, the real
estate boards. Only a very small number of nonwhite brokers have
been admitted to these associations in a few cities. Their exclusion testifies to the racial attitudes of the real estate fraternity
and symbolizes the separate housing market for minority groups.
Exclusion is regarded by these groups as an arbitrary denial of
opportunities for wider business and professional contacts and
facilities which the trade associations provide for their members.

There are consequences for the general public as well. One result is the absence of communication between white and nonwhite
interests in the real estate field. Many of the problems constantly
arising around race in the real estate field might be susceptible of
easier adjustment if the interests involved had the opportunity of
communicating with each other. From the standpoint of preserving the *status quo* in race relations, however, communication
would probably be a disadvantage, since it would lead necessarily
to the posing of alternatives. The real estate boards, by excluding
nonwhites, insulate themselves from the possibility of having to
listen to the minority point of view. Another consequence of exclusion is to remove nonwhite real estate agents from the scope of
ethical practice controls which the real estate boards endeavor to
exercise with respect to their members and the real estate business

generally. Real estate boards place considerable emphasis on their functions of raising standards in the real estate business and protecting the public from unethical practices, but this protection is not extended to those sections of the public served by brokers who are not white.

Builders

Racial segregation is much more complete in new housing developments than in established neighborhoods. Among the latter, though barriers to nonwhite entry are often strong, they are seldom absolute because no one has complete control of the situation. Even in the most exclusive neighborhoods there may be some nonconformist seller or broker who will refuse to hold the line. In a new housing tract, on the other hand, a single management controls, at least initially, the occupancy of all houses in the tract. Except as limited by law in certain states and cities, the vast majority of private builders [10] in all sections of the country maintain a strict policy of racial segregation. These builders permit nonwhites to buy or rent only in developments specifically intended for minority occupancy. Since there are comparatively few of these, the result is to exclude nonwhites from the larger and better part of the new housing supply.

Changes in the house-building industry during the past twenty years have magnified the power of private builders to shape the character of communities. So long as house building was small-scale business, no single builder could greatly affect the nature of residential districts to which he might add a few units. With the transition of house building to a large volume, mass-production industry, the modern tract developer builds not just houses but communities. He has acquired the power to determine, for whole communities, not only the racial pattern but many other aspects of community life. Throughout the country, many new communities have come into existence into which no single Negro has been admitted, by policy of the private builders. In creating thousands of housing developments exclusively for whites, and some

[10] This discussion is based on interviews with some 200 builders in various sections of the country, reported more fully in *Residence and Race*, Chapter 11: "The House Building Industry," and in the special study by N. J. Demerath and Associates, *Private Enterprise Housing for Negroes in Seven Metropolitan Areas* (see Appendix).

scores of others wholly for nonwhites, the private building industry has done much to intensify racial segregation.

The expanded power of private builders and the use of their power in the manner described go far to explain the paradox of increasing residential segregation during a period of generally weakening racial prejudice and discrimination. Builders, no doubt, are on the whole no more prejudiced racially than they were twenty years ago, but changed conditions in the production and marketing of housing have given greater scope to their racial decisions.

In sales housing, of course, builder control of occupancy usually terminates with the initial sales. Resales in most developments are at the discretion of the individual home owners. However, once a pattern of racial exclusion has been established through an entire community, many interests solidify in its support, and it becomes extremely difficult to change.

The rationale of builders in the North and West for racial exclusion runs mainly in terms of business necessity. In the first place, many builders report that financial institutions and local governments insist upon racial segregation as a condition for their coöperation in home-building enterprises. According to these reports, a builder who proposed to admit nonwhites to a development in a white area would be stopped by inability to obtain financing or by the refusal of local government authorities to grant necessary permits and approvals, or by both. Actually, few builders have tested their assumptions in this area, but it is, nevertheless, a commonly stated belief.

Most builders share with real estate brokers and others the conviction that whites will not live in the same neighborhoods with nonwhites, or at least that the number of whites who will do so is not large enough to provide a sufficient market for a new housing development. For this reason, builders are generally convinced that to admit nonwhites would be a fatal handicap to sales. Builders point out that a successful housing tract operation requires a rapid rate of sales with a complete sellout. It is said that a builder makes his profit on a particular development from the last 10 percent of houses sold. Therefore, a development which sells slowly or fails to sell out completely within a reasonable time is a commercial failure. A nondiscriminatory policy is considered a business risk which the large majority of builders have determined not to undertake.

In addition to these business calculations, many builders undoubtedly favor segregation on principle. In the South especially, interracial housing is never considered except as an alternative to be fought. Some leading builders have publicly advocated expansion of segregated building for Negroes as a means of forestalling pressures for open occupancy in private housing.

A few builders, in various parts of the country, have ventured to challenge the racial assumptions and practices of the industry and offer their products to an unsegregated market. Their experience, reported elsewhere in detail,[11] has confirmed the existence of strong opposition to interracial housing by other builders, real estate and financial interests, and local government. Opposition has been focused against the introduction of nonwhites into areas considered to be for whites only. Mortgage lenders, in addition, have questioned the existence of a sufficient market for interracial housing. Nondiscriminatory builders have usually met the opposition, not by collision, but by seeking sites where the presence of nonwhites would meet with least objection. There is evidence of some moderation of the opposition to interracial housing, particularly by financial institutions, but there is still a long way to go in this direction. Lenders have been encouraged to a more receptive attitude toward interracial housing by the change in policy of the Federal Housing Administration, discussed below.

With respect to the salability of housing in interracial developments, experience to date has not provided a wholly unbiased test because of builders' enforced frequent use of less attractive sites. Sales have often been somewhat slower than in comparable (but better situated) all-white developments, but with few exceptions, open-occupancy builders have been able to sell out profitably to an interracial market. Where a good housing value has been offered, together with evidence that the community was genuinely interracial and not a Negro development euphemistically called interracial or open, whites have proved willing to buy.

[11] Eunice and George Grier, *Privately Developed Interracial Housing: An Analysis of Experience* (see Appendix).

Financial Institutions

Mortgage-lending institutions have provided major support for racial segregation by their common policy of lending to nonwhites only in certain areas and refusing to finance the purchase of housing by nonwhites in white neighborhoods. Most lenders insist that they make no racial or color distinctions in the granting of loans, and as evidence many can show substantial portfolios of loans to nonwhites. The restriction of nonwhite borrowers to certain racial districts, nevertheless, is a serious form of discrimination. Not only does it serve to sustain segregation, but it disadvantages nonwhites in the terms of mortgage credit because the properties in the areas where they are permitted to buy are generally inferior risks from a lender's standpoint.

A "racial areas" policy is not universal among lending institutions, and there are variations in the strictness with which it is applied. Two principal justifications for the policy are advanced by lenders who adhere to it. One is the belief that nonwhite entry into white neighborhoods damages property values and hence the security of real estate investments. The other is public relations, a desire to avoid the wrath of property owners, brokers, depositors, and policy holders, and other lenders for helping to "break" a white neighborhood.

In recent years, lenders' belief in the property-values theory seems to have weakened considerably and, in consequence, the public relations motive has become, for many lenders, the chief basis for withholding loans to nonwhites in white neighborhoods. The shift of emphasis is important because factors of public relations do not exert a uniform force in all areas nor upon all lenders. Moreover, there is usually room for differing judgments about the extent of adverse reaction to a particular loan and probable consequences for the lending institution. As a result, lender policy on the issue has tended to become vague and variable.

Government

The policies and actions of government agencies and public officials must be counted among the principal influences sustaining racial segregation in housing. As the United Nations Subcommission on Prevention of Discrimination and Protection of Minorities has said, "The most serious forms of discrimination are those embodied in laws and regulations . . . [and] those practiced by authorities and public officials."

Federal housing agencies.—The Federal government, through its mortgage credit aids, public housing, and slum clearance programs, has come to exercise a large measure of control over housing. Both directly and indirectly, the Federal housing programs have strongly influenced the racial patterns of residence, mainly in the direction of increasing racial segregation. During the first dozen years of its existence, the Federal Housing Administration operated explicitly on the real estate doctrine that mingling of racial groups in residence areas was socially undesirable and a threat to the financial stability of neighborhoods. Its appraisal manuals stressed the importance of protecting neighborhoods against invasion by "incompatible racial and social groups." For "surest protection" against such an eventuality, FHA recommended blanketing all land in the vicinity of a mortgage-insured housing development with race-restrictive covenants, particularly in undeveloped or partly developed areas. It is a fair judgment that FHA's influence contributed largely to the spread of race-restrictive covenants (subsequently declared unenforceable by the Supreme Court) and hence to the exclusion of minority groups from wide areas.

In the postwar period, FHA has abandoned its earlier racial policy and declared for "equality of opportunity to receive the benefits of the mortgage insurance system . . . irrespective of race, color, creed, or national origin." [12] The agency now officially encourages open occupancy in housing developments, but it does not attempt to control the discriminatory practices of private builders or lenders.

The public housing program has always insisted, and in the main successfully, on minority groups' receiving an equitable share of publicly subsidized dwellings. With respect to the racial pattern, Federal policy has been to leave the decision for open or segregated occupancy to local housing authorities. The latter, in

---

[12] Federal Housing Administration, "Message from FHA Commissioner to be Read by Insuring Office Directors at NAHB Local Meetings Relating to Providing Homes Available to Minorities," July 16, 1954.

all sections of the country, elected initially for segregation, with one or two notable exceptions. In the South, compulsory segregation remains, but in the North and West, many local authorities have shifted to policies of open occupancy, some by their own decision, others under court order. In this movement, public housing has been and remains far in advance of the private field. The earliest, and still the majority, of planned housing communities open to qualified tenants without racial barriers are public housing projects. Notwithstanding open-occupancy policies, however, the recent trend has been running strongly toward concentration of minority groups in public housing. Among the major factors contributing to this trend are the frequent location of projects in areas mainly occupied by minorities, the wider opportunities of whites than of nonwhites to obtain housing in the private market, and statutory preference in tenant selection to families, largely minority, displaced by slum clearance operations. Without discounting the earnest efforts by some local housing authorities to develop racially integrated patterns, but considering all factors, the conclusion seems justified that public housing has served, on the whole, to sustain and probably intensify racial segregation.

Beginning during World War II, the Federal government has become increasingly sensitive to the housing disadvantage and needs of the minority groups. It has moved to assist these groups to obtain housing but has tried to do so without interfering with the segregation practices of the private housing industry. In wartime, housing for nonwhite (as well as white) war workers was programmed, and a share of materials priorities was allocated to it. Special staffs of "Race Relations Advisors" have been set up in the housing agencies. Special credit assistance has been provided through the Federal National Mortgage Association and the Voluntary Home Mortgage Credit Program. The result of these provisions has been to stimulate a volume of new construction for minorities, not large, perhaps, in relation to the need, but much greater than private industry would otherwise have provided. A high proportion of all postwar new dwellings built for minority use has been financed by mortgages purchased by the FNMA, that is, by government credit. These new houses have been built, with few exceptions, in segregated projects. The special assistance measures, therefore, like public housing, have been both a source of housing and a force for segregation.

Indirectly, Federal policies have stimulated segregation in two important ways. The changes in the housing industry which have so largely increased the power of private builders to determine community patterns, as described above, have been made possible by the Federal mortgage insurance systems. The FHA and VA policies of giving commitments to insure the mortgages on entire housing tracts in advance of construction provide the necessary basis for corresponding advance commitments of financing by lending institutions, thus enabling builders to construct hundreds and even thousands of houses for subsequent sale. FNMA advance commitments to purchase mortgages have supplemented this system, providing assurance of financing for housing projects at a disadvantage in the commercial money market. Without Federal mortgage aids, housing tract building operations could not have developed to anything like their scale in the postwar years.

The other indirect Federal support of segregation has been the moral sanction given to the racial discrimination practices of private business. As Myrdal has said, "It is one thing when private tenants, property owners, and financial institutions maintain and extend patterns of racial segregation in housing. It is quite another matter when a Federal agency chooses to side with the segregationists." Government, as an expression of the public will, is one of the sources of moral as well as legal authority. If the government sees nothing wrong in racial discrimination, how can private persons be censured for practicing it? In some fields, notably the armed forces, the government has actively moved to abolish segregation. In the housing field, the Federal government, in recent years, has withdrawn from any explicit endorsement of housing segregation. Federal agencies, however, aside from verbal pronouncements for equality, continue to tolerate the discriminatory practices of those who distribute Federal benefits.

Local governments.—Municipal governments, in the past, have repeatedly endeavored to enforce segregation upon racial minority groups by law. All such measures, whenever they could be brought under judicial review, have been declared unconstitutional. Racial zoning ordinances were invalidated by the Supreme Court in 1917, but at least one large city—Birmingham, Alabama—nevertheless continued to pass and enforce racial zoning laws in the 1950's.[13]

Local housing authorities in many cases, both in the South and elsewhere, have enforced by administrative procedure a more rigid racial segregation in public housing than existed in private neighborhoods. In many southern cities, New Orleans for example, whites and Negroes have historically lived interspersed throughout a considerable part of the city, but in public housing the local authorities have established complete segregation.[14]

In ways not accessible to judicial review, local public agencies and officials, particularly in suburban communities, frequently use their discretionary powers over land use and building to prevent the entry of minority groups into areas reserved for white occupancy. Zoning classifications may be changed, land may be condemned for public use, or necessary official approvals may be withheld. In the South, these official actions are often quite open, although illegal, but in the North and West the discriminatory purpose is customarily concealed behind other announced motives. Because the motives are concealed, it is not possible to know exactly how extensive the practices are, but there is evidence of frequent abuse of governmental powers to restrict the housing opportunities of nonwhite minorities. Builders who have attempted or considered projects either for open occupancy or for minorities consistently describe the policies of local governments as one of the major factors restraining the use of land for those purposes.[15]

ADDENDUM

Implications that real estate brokers, builders, and financial institutions, as a group, favor and promote discriminatory practices in housing may be justified in regard to individuals but are not warranted in regard to those occupational groups as such. These people do not originate policies, discriminatory or otherwise, in the operation of the projects they negotiate or finance.

The value of anything, including land and buildings, is subjective. If real estate

[13] Birmingham's recent efforts to control the residence of Negroes by zoning and other legal devices are described in Thompson, Lewis, and McEntire, *Southern Approaches to Housing for Negroes* (see Appendix). A brief history of municipal legal measures to establish residential segregation is given in *Residence and Race*, Chapter 15: "Race Discrimination and the Law."

[14] Forrest E. LaViolette, with the assistance of Joseph T. Taylor and Giles Hubert, *Negro Housing in the New Orleans Community* (see Appendix).

[15] Further discussion and instances are given in *Residence and Race*, Chapter 15: "Race Discrimination and the Law"; Thompson, Lewis, and McEntire, *Southern Approaches to Housing for Negroes;* and Eunice and George Grier, *Privately Developed Interracial Housing: An Analysis of Experience* (see Appendix).

investors believe, rightly or wrongly, that integrated occupancy does impair values, that belief, widely enough held, will of itself impair values. That this is now true, no one who looks at the situation fairly and is competent to judge will deny.

Brokers, builders, and lenders handle their businesses in ways which reveal that in some areas the belief in the possibility of such impairment is widely enough held to be an obstacle to negotiations and a threat to the stability of values.

Except in those cases where real estate brokers affirmatively encourage, rather than reflect, the belief that integrated occupancy impairs values, they cannot fairly be held responsible for a situation which might better be handled by changing the thinking of a community, which is after all, the basis of opposition to integrated occupancy.
—PETER GRIMM

Chapter 3

SOCIAL AND ECONOMIC CONSEQUENCES OF RESIDENTIAL SEGREGATION

The exclusion of persons from residence areas because of their race, color, creed, or ethnic attachment is a deprivation of personal freedom of a particularly vital kind—the liberty to move and to choose a place of residence according to one's needs, tastes, and ability to pay. There is, of course, no absolute freedom of residence choice for anyone. Individual choices are always limited by law and by economic considerations. But racial or ethnic discrimination imposes on the subject groups special and additional restrictions. These restrictions violate fundamental principles of American democracy and Judeo-Christian morality. Compulsory racial or ethnic segregation is, therefore, inherently wrong, regardless of the consequences which can be traced to it. However, segregation does have many damaging consequences, both for the segregated groups and for the general public and nation.

Consequences for the Segregated Groups

Residential and other forms of segregation.—The residential segregation of a minority group leads directly to segregation in other areas of life: schools, churches, hospitals, places of public accommodations, recreation, and welfare and civic activities. Although compulsory segregation in public schools has been declared unlawful by the Supreme Court, many schools in the North and West are actually segregated, not by law but in consequence of the racial pattern of residence.

Segregated social institutions restrict personal contacts across racial lines between persons of similar interest. Professional workers and business men of the segregated group, limited to clients in the "ghetto," are turned inward toward their racial group rather than outward toward their occupational and business groups. Of all factors tending to isolate nonwhite minorities and impede their participation in the general community life, residential segregation is without doubt the most important.

Segregation and discrimination.—Compulsory segregation is itself discrimination, but it also exposes the segregated group to other forms of discrimination. When a group is set apart spatially, it becomes very easy to neglect their needs or to discriminate against them. The facility of discrimination is accentuated when, as in many parts of the South, the segregated group is also disfranchised and has no way of influencing public policy or public officials in the normal democratic way. One of the outstanding characteristics of minority residential areas is the inferior quality of public services including police protection, sanitation, street and sidewalk maintenance, and housing code enforcement. The public neglect of Negro districts is notorious in the South and is common throughout the country.

Housing market effects.—The restriction of minority groups to limited areas and, in cities of the North and West, the accompanying increase of minority populations, together result in chronic, severe scarcity of housing available to segregated groups. This leads in turn to overcrowding of dwelling space, doubling of families, and the subdivision of dwellings into smaller units (conversions). Moreover, the housing in the areas where minorities are permitted to live is in great part old and of poor quality. A striking consequence is that segregated groups receive less housing value for their dollars spent than do whites, by a wide margin. Census statistics indicate that at every level of rent or market value, nonwhite renters and home owners obtain fewer standard quality dwellings and frequently less space than do whites paying the same amounts.[1]

Nonwhites purchasing homes receive, on the whole, less favorable terms of mortgage credit than do white home buyers. This is due not so much to direct discrimination by lending institutions as to the poorer quality of the nonwhites' properties, a handicap deriving from segregation. Many mortgage lenders will not loan at all in blighted areas. Those who do ordinarily demand higher interest rates, larger down payments, and shorter repayment periods than in good quality districts.[2]

[1] A more detailed analysis is presented in *Residence and Race*, Chapter 9: "Housing Quality and Cost."

[2] See *Residence and Race*, Chapter 13: "Mortgage Financing."

For similar reasons, segregation also deprives nonwhites of equal participation in the benefits of government housing programs. Housing conforming to FHA insured loan standards is very scarce in the slums and blighted areas, and nonwhites are not permitted to live in the areas where most government-aided housing is being built.

Barriers to social progress.[3]—The traditional individualistic response of Americans to an undesirable situation has been to move away from it. The migration of Negroes from rural areas and away from the South is in this tradition. But when they find themselves caught in a city slum, their avenues of escape are blocked by segregation. Not just in a negative but in a positive sense, mobility has always been one of the principal avenues in America for individual advancement. Its denial to nonwhites, as concerns residence, greatly handicaps the efforts of individuals to improve their circumstances.

In even more basic ways, segregation tends to obstruct the avenues of advancement for segregated groups. On the way to fuller participation and higher status in American life, the members of these groups have a great deal to learn. In addition to a low level of general education and a limited development of occupational skills, large sections of the Negro, Puerto Rican, and Mexican-American populations are unfamiliar with many of the values, standards, and accepted ways of behaving in the urban environment. In a phrase, like many immigrant groups before them, they are culturally unassimilated.

To develop culturally is a learning process, but learning depends upon experiences, contacts, and opportunities, as well as on the motivation of expected rewards. Formal education is, of course, crucially important, but social learning comes from many sources other than the schools. People learn ways of behaving by example and, above all, by participation. The isolation of a group from the larger community both deprives its members of learning opportunities and insulates them against pressures to learn, thus retarding the normal processes of cultural development.

---

[3] This discussion of social and psychological consequences of segregation draws heavily from a research memorandum prepared for the Commission in the Department of Social Sciences, Fisk University, summarizing the findings of pertinent research. Jitsuichi Masuoka and Preston Valien, *Social Consequences of Racial Residential Segregation* (see Appendix).

Psychological effects.—Psychologists are generally agreed that compulsory segregation has harmful psychological effects on the segregated groups. Arbitrary interference with an individual's pursuit of what he considers, and is socially encouraged to consider, a legitimate goal (such as better housing) produces feelings of frustration, hopelessness, and hostility. When minority families are prevented from moving into better homes and neighborhoods as their incomes rise, a normal incentive to self-improvement is taken away. They become habituated to a low standard of housing, and their aspirations for something better are curtailed.

As an unceasing reminder of inferior status, segregation and the discrimination that goes with it are damaging to the personality development of minority children. Many, particularly adolescents, develop feelings of inferiority and doubts of their personal worth, and they fail to develop strong motivations to achievement.

Disorganization of family life, common among Negroes of the lower class, results from a historical complex of factors of which housing conditions are only one. However, one of the consequences of segregation has been to compel many Negro families to occupy quarters poorly adapted to family needs. The crowded conditions in many Negro households and the lack of suitable space and facilities for family living have unquestionably contributed to the instability of Negro family ties.

Consequences for the General Community and the Nation

Loss of potential skills and talent.—Segregation handicaps the members of minority groups and obstructs their economic and social progress. When individuals are denied opportunity or stimulus to develop their potentialities, it is not they alone who suffer, but the whole community as well, because it is deprived of contributions which the disadvantaged persons might otherwise make. The community's interest in the development of all its members lies at the basis of the public school system and the large expenditures of public funds for education at all levels. In the present world, few will deny that the security and welfare of the United States demand realization of the potential of its human resources to the fullest extent. Hence, racial segregation and related conditions which impede the development of a large section of the population—one-sixth of the total—impose a handicap on the nation which cannot with safety be ignored.[4]

Segregation and slums.—One of the principal social problems confronting American cities is the persistence and growth of slums. Many cities are clearing and rebuilding their slum areas with financial assistance from the Federal program of urban renewal, but there is evidence that slums may be growing faster than they can be removed under this slow-moving program.

The problems of slum clearance and urban renewal are seriously aggravated by residential segregation. Urban renewal plans usually contemplate the re-use of slum areas, after rebuilding, by higher income groups than previously occupied them, or re-use for non-residential purposes, or both. Sound planning, also, in many cases requires substantial reduction of population densities. The result is that all or part of the renewal area population must be relocated elsewhere. When the slum residents are minority groups, as to a large and increasing extent they are, their relocation becomes very difficult because of the limited alternatives available to them.

Municipal agencies in charge of urban renewal are seldom prepared to challenge racial segregation, although this is the main obstacle to finding alternative housing for minority groups displaced from slums. But to relocate the excess population in other slum or blighted areas intensifies the crowding there, while threatening an over-all net reduction in the living space available to minorities.

Persons concerned with minority rights have been critical of urban renewal programs because of their tendency to remove minorities from certain areas without opening up adequate alternative opportunities for residence. For this reason, slum clearance is sometimes called "Negro clearance," and Charles Abrams asserts that urban redevelopment has been "deflected from its original social reform course and pointed toward ousting minorities."

[4] The words of one student of the problem of utilizing the potentialities of the Negro population are worth quoting. Concerned mainly with education and occupational preparation, this author writes: "It must be recognized that the Negro cannot suddenly take his place among whites in the adult world of work if he has never lived, played, and studied with them in childhood and young adulthood. Any type of segregation handicaps a person's preparation for work and life. . . . Only when Negro and white families can live together as neighbors, when Negro and white children can play together, study together, go to the same church—only then will the Negro grow up properly prepared for his place in the world of work." Eli Ginzberg, *The Negro Potential* (New York: Columbia University Press, 1956), pp. 114-115.

The problem has been pointedly stated by the Administrator of the Housing and Home Finance Agency, in the following terms:

> Regardless of what measures are provided or developed to clear slums and meet low-income housing needs, the critical factor in the situation which must be met is the fact of racial exclusion from the greater and better part of our housing supply. . . . No program of housing or urban improvement, however well conceived, well financed, or comprehensive, can hope to make more than indifferent progress until we open up adequate opportunities to minority families for decent housing.[5]

Apart from urban renewal problems, the expansion of residence areas open to minority groups frequently takes place in a manner and under circumstances conducive to the formation of slums. Properties tend to be overused and abused, housing space is subdivided into smaller units, maintenance is neglected, public services and law enforcement deteriorate.

When a person acquires a home in a neighborhood, he typically moves into an established social situation and normally conforms to the neighborhood standards. A good neighborhood is usually an organized one, at least informally, and often formally with a property owners' association or similar organization. A family that fails to maintain its house or control its children according to neighborhood standards will be brought under social pressures to conform. The organized neighborhood is also usually alert to maintaining a proper standard of municipal services and to opposing unwanted types of building.

When occupants of a neighborhood are more or less completely replaced by a new group, the neighborhood's system of standards and social controls is likely to be swept away, particularly if the transition takes place rapidly. The new occupants may form their own system of social controls, but time is needed for this because they come as individuals, not as an organized group. In the meantime, the neighborhood may deteriorate slightly or greatly. If the incoming group is culturally advanced, the quality of the neighborhood is likely to suffer little if at all. But if, as is more common, the newcomers belong to a lower socio-economic group, a marked decline of housing standards is probable. Age and condition of the houses involved are, of course, also important factors in determining the outcome.

[5] Albert M. Cole, "What Is the Federal Government's Role in Housing?" Address to the Economic Club of Detroit, February 8, 1954.

The deterioration of housing and neighborhood conditions which often occurs with racial transition is not racially caused but results from the nature of the transition process itself, the socio-economic status of the groups involved, and the character of the properties. Where individual minority families have been able to acquire homes in good neighborhoods without setting in motion a process of racial transition, surveys indicate that they have been absorbed without disturbance to neighborhood standards.

A stimulant to prejudice.—If racial segregation is sustained by race prejudice, it is equally true that segregation is, itself, a major stimulant to prejudice. Group prejudice is basically a habit of looking upon members of certain groups not as individuals but as groups, and attributing the same characteristics to all. Isolation of a group and consequent reduction of personal contacts between its members and others obviously reinforces this tendency. Most white people have very little opportunity to learn what Negroes, for example, are really like as persons. Contacts of whites with Negroes are nearly always limited and formal and usually involve unequal status, with the Negroes in the position of employees, servants, or service workers. Several studies have shown that interracial contacts on an equal status basis are conducive to a reduction of prejudice, especially when the contacts are based on common interests.[6] Under a regime of segregation, however, contacts of this type are rare.

The fact that segregation minimizes opportunities for experience with individuals almost inevitably leads to superficial group observation and judgments. It is easy to see, for example, that the worst housing sections in town are full of Negroes or Puerto Ricans or Mexicans. Since type of house and neighborhood carry fairly definite implications about personal worth and status, those who live in disreputable neighborhoods are readily judged to be low status people.

Also, in some specific ways, segregation stimulates group antag-

[6] Relevant studies are examined in the research reports by Claire Selltiz and Stuart W. Cook, and by Helen E. Amerman (see Appendix). An important study demonstrating the effects on racial attitudes of shared experiences and community of interest is Robert K. Merton, Patricia S. West, and Marie Jahoda, *Social Facts and Social Fictions: The Dynamics of Race Relations in Hilltown* (New York: Columbia University, Bureau of Applied Social Research, 1949, hectographed); part of a larger work by the same authors to be published under the title, *Patterns of Social Life: Explorations in the Social Psychology and Sociology of Housing.*

onisms. The pressure of a segregated group to expand its residence boundaries is perceived by the residents of near-by areas as a threat. Thus the competition of people for housing, which otherwise is an economic and marketing problem, is transformed by segregation into a source of social conflict.

Foreign relations.—The problem of racial inequality in the United States is no longer a purely domestic issue; it vitally affects the foreign relations of the country. One of the stakes in the struggle between the free world and the communist bloc is the allegiance of the so-called "uncommitted peoples," almost all of whom are nonwhite. In this phase of the world contest, the United States is seriously handicapped by the continued practice of racial segregation and discrimination within its borders. The rising colored nations of Asia and Africa show extreme sensitivity about their status in the world. Any evidence that white people regard or treat nonwhites as inferiors is fiercely resented, and race relations in the United States and South Africa constantly provide that evidence. The fact that nonwhites are compelled to live apart from the white population, in separate and usually inferior districts, is a glaring example.

Few aspects of American life are more highly publicized throughout the world than racial discrimination. Communist anti-American propaganda plays tirelessly on the racial theme, and this attack is difficult to counter because of the element of truth in its allegations. Such dramatic episodes as the violent exclusion of Negro children from the high school at Little Rock do grave damage to the prestige of the United States abroad, as President Eisenhower stated; and every action that deprives individuals, because of their race or color, of rights and privileges enjoyed by others, in some measure burdens the nation in the world struggle.

Chapter 4

TOWARD EQUALITY OF OPPORTUNITY

Various measures have been taken to reduce racial discrimination and promote equality of rights and opportunities. An appraisal of these measures will provide a basis for considering what further steps might be recommended. Reference is particularly but not exclusively to the field of housing and residence. Housing is not independent of other aspects of life; discriminatory barriers in this field are part of the larger pattern of racial and ethnic discrimination. Almost any measure that serves to widen the opportunities open to the disadvantaged groups and improve their social and economic conditions will tend in some degree to weaken the residence barriers.

Back of the specific actions to promote equality stand two major social trends: the rising economic status of the minority groups and the reawakened concern of the general public with the problem of racial inequality. These trends have provided stimulus to action and a growing public readiness to accept changes. Specific measures have included judicial decisions, legislation, governmental administrative action, private industry ventures in open-occupancy housing, and a variety of proequality activities by private or semipublic organizations.

Judicial Decisions

A great deal of the discrimination in the past against minority groups, especially Negroes, has been created and enforced by law and by discriminatory administration of law. For many years legal segregation was sustained by the courts under the doctrine of "separate but equal." Beginning about 1935, the Supreme Court became increasingly critical of segregation laws, culminating in the famous school decisions of 1954 wherein the Court determined that, as applied to education, segregation was "inherently unequal."

In housing, the Supreme Court has never been willing to justify segregation as separate but equal. More than four decades ago, the Court settled decisively that local governments could not establish racial residential segregation by law. In 1948, the Court extended this principle to restrain courts, as branches of government, from enforcing private agreements for racial segregation.

In the nature of the judicial review function, the role of the Supreme Court in promoting equal rights is to restrain legislatures, courts, and public officials from discriminating against minority groups. This is a function of the greatest importance because of the power of government, if not checked, to sustain and legitimize discrimination. Many discriminatory laws and administrative procedures still stand; but if the logic of the Supreme Court's recent decisions is applied generally, it will mean that, so far as judicial review extends, the power of government cannot be used to maintain any form of racial segregation or discrimination. Thus discrimination will be deprived, as it largely is already, of what formerly was one of its most effective sanctions.

State and Municipal Legislation

If law can be used to enforce discrimination, it can also be employed to promote equal rights.[1] The movement for racial equality during the past dozen years has relied heavily on legislation. Many states and municipalities have adopted laws prohibiting discrimination in employment, housing, public accommodations, education, and other areas. At the end of 1957, sixteen states and fifteen cities had legislated or officially resolved for equal rights in some aspect of housing. Almost all of this legislation applies to housing which is affected with some public character. The most comprehensive laws, with one exception, are those in force in six states—Connecticut, Massachusetts, New Jersey, New York, Oregon, and Washington—prohibiting discrimination in all publicly assisted housing including housing developments built with government mortgage insurance. The exception is New York City's law applying to all housing (public and private) in multiple-unit structures and to new sales housing in ten or more units.

[1] An extended analysis of the uses of law, both to sustain discrimination and to promote equal rights, is contained in *Residence and Race*, Chapter 15: "Race Discrimination and the Law."

This is the first law aimed at prohibiting racial or ethnic discrimination in the housing market generally.

Many people doubt the possibility of promoting racial equality by law. It is often said that social customs cannot be changed by legislation, and also that law cannot change the attitudes that are the basis of the race problem. The failure of prohibition is cited, also the failure of the Federal civil rights laws enacted after the Civil War and the nonenforcement of state laws against discrimination in public accommodations adopted during the latter part of the last century. These legislative failures are enough to demonstrate that mere passage of a law is no infallible cure for a social evil, but they do not justify a conclusion that law is of no avail.

Most contemporary students of the subject hold that law *can be* a potent force for changing social habits and indirectly can modify attitudes. Laws against racial discrimination, even when running counter to customary practice, are consistent with the moral and political ideals held by most Americans and may expect public support for that reason. Moreover, it is essential to note that American laws in this field, as in others, do not require any persons to hold or change any attitudes but only to refrain from certain acts (discrimination). Although attitudes of race prejudice are undoubtedly basic factors in the situation, as previously pointed out, they do not control action in any simple or uniform way. Prejudiced persons do not always discriminate, and unprejudiced persons sometimes do discriminate. The situation in which a person finds himself is a major determinant of his behavior, and the situation can be changed by law.

A great deal of psychological research has demonstrated that a person's attitudes are largely shaped by experiences and factors in his environment.[2] Attitudes of race prejudice, like other commonly held attitudes, are nourished and supported by environmental conditions. Law can weaken or sometimes remove the environmental supports and thereby lead to a change in attitudes. One of the major supports to race prejudice is discrimination itself and the results of discrimination. Hence action that prevents discrimination will lead to a reduction of racial prejudice.

[2] The evidence is analyzed in Selltiz and Cook, *Studies in the Social Psychology of Race and Housing* (see Appendix).

Whether a law will be effective in preventing discrimination depends, obviously, upon its enforcement. Until recent years, state laws against discrimination (mainly the public accommodation statutes) made no feasible provision for enforcement and afforded no practical remedy for an aggrieved person. Lacking enforcement machinery, the older laws remained dead letters on the statute books. Recent antidiscrimination laws, in contrast, are not only broader than the older statutes, but they also incorporate a distinctive philosophy and method of enforcement.

The framers and the administrators of the modern equal rights legislation regard law and education not as alternative but as complementary methods of promoting equality. Together with the statutory restraints, an educational program is written into most, if not all, of the laws as a major reliance for securing public acceptance of the legislation and compliance with its provisions. Most of the laws in the different states have been modeled after those of New York and are, for this reason, quite similar, even to the point of much identical language. They have in common four essential features. First is administration by a special commission or agency. Experience has demonstrated that legal control of discrimination, to be effective, requires special administrative procedures. Second, when complaints of unlawful discrimination are received, the commission investigates the facts; if evidence of discrimination is found, it attempts by conference and conciliation to persuade the offender to comply with the law. These proceedings are informal and unpublicized. Third, if informal conciliation efforts fail, the commission invokes formal procedures, holds a public hearing, may issue a cease and desist order, and if the order is disregarded, apply to the courts for enforcement. Fourth is provision for a program of public information and education designed to create public understanding and acceptance of the law and to generate a public opinion favorable to compliance.

The formal sanctions provided by the laws have been very little used. The great majority of discrimination complaints have been settled by informal methods of investigation and conference. In essence, therefore, administrative commissions have relied upon voluntary compliance. Nevertheless, the existence of legal sanctions in the background is considered essential. The commissions

are engaged mainly in a work of persuasion, yet it is not pure
persuasion. The supporters of equal rights legislation are strongly
convinced that the commissions, to be effective, must have authority and sanctions at their disposal, even if they use them spar-
ingly.

The administrative procedures described were initially developed in relation to fair employment legislation. As other nondiscrimination laws have been enacted, they have been placed
under the jurisdiction of the commissions and administered in
the same way. The housing laws are the most recent legislation
of this general kind; most of them were adopted only during the
past two or three years.

It is difficult to evaluate the effects of modern antidiscrimination laws with any precision. In employment and use of public
accommodations, a significant reduction of discrimination has
occurred during the period in which the laws have been in effect.
The laws, of course, have been only one of several factors operat-
ing to produce this result. The commissions can be credited with
breaking through a number of barriers at strategic points, such
as opening employment opportunities for minorities with some
leading employers and in certain occupations formerly closed to
them. The role of the commissions in opening opportunities will
be particularly important in housing. The laws and commissions
have afforded new opportunities and programs for community
education which otherwise would not have existed. On the whole,
it is the consensus of observers that the laws have played a significant, if not measurable, role in the decline of racial discrimination during the past decade or two.

The effects of the housing laws on racial residence patterns
during the brief period of their existence do not afford a sufficient
basis for firm judgment. Indications are that effects depend very
much on the location and price of the housing developments
affected. Except in the vicinity of existing areas of minority concentration, legal removal of discriminatory barriers seems to result in a rather thin scatter of minority families instead of new
concentrations. In New York, several coöperative housing developments built under long-standing nondiscriminatory law for
this type of housing, but at a considerable distance from Harlem,
have attracted only 5 to 10 percent of Negroes in their popula-

tions. Developments built on slum-cleared land in Manhattan have been more attractive to Negroes, but even here higher-priced developments have been occupied by Negroes only to the extent of around 25 percent. These experiences illustrate two central facts about minority housing demand as previously described: only a small proportion of minority families are able to pay for new, good quality dwellings at current prices; and, under existing conditions, comparatively few nonwhite families seem to be interested in moving far from the minority community. These conditions may change, of course, and the long-period prospect may well be quite different from the short run. For the present, however, nondiscrimination laws have not called forth a large demand from minorities for new development housing, and there seems to be no reason to expect it. When the demand which does exist is spread over a great number of projects and locations, the effect on any single location is obviously slight.

Fears expressed by some that nondiscrimination laws would disrupt the housing industry, causing lenders to withhold mortgage funds and discourage sales, have not been realized in the states which have adopted such legislation. No substantial complaints of economic loss have been made. In fact, real fears of destructive consequences have evidently not been widespread, since in several states the laws were enacted with little opposition. In the state of Washington, for example, a law very similar to that of New York, prohibiting discrimination in the marketing of FHA-, VA-, and other government-assisted housing, passed the lower house of the legislature without a dissenting vote and the state senate by an overwhelming majority.

Federal Administrative Action

Until the Civil Rights Act of 1957, the national Congress had enacted no legislation touching domestic minority group relations since 1875. Presidents, however, and agencies of the Federal government have taken various executive and administrative actions aimed at securing equal treatment of citizens in their relations with the government. Without doubt, the most far-reaching executive action of this kind, in terms of its implications, has been the abolition of racial segregation in the armed forces. During World War II, an executive order created a Fair Employment

Practices Commission, the first action by any branch of government to promote racial equality of opportunity for employment. Subsequently, a series of executive orders was issued to provide for nondiscriminatory employment on government contracts.

In housing, as previously mentioned, the FHA has several times amended and rewritten its property-appraisal standards to cleanse them of racial criteria. It has announced an open-occupancy policy on sales and rentals of housing acquired by the agency. The Public Housing Administration has evolved a "racial equity formula" and other administrative procedures to assure nonwhites an equitable share of public housing units.

The major racial issue in the housing programs of the Federal government is how far the government should go in controlling the discriminatory practices of private business and local public agencies in the distribution of Federal housing benefits. The Federal agencies have largely if not completely eliminated racial discrimination so far as their own internal operations are concerned. But very little housing or housing aids are distributed by the Federal government directly to the ultimate recipients. As a matter of fundamental policy, Federal housing programs operate through private industry or local public authorities.

Minority advancement and equal rights organizations have for years strongly urged the President and the Federal housing agencies to proscribe discrimination in the marketing of houses built with government assistance. This step the Federal government has not been prepared to take. Officials offer various explanations, but unquestionably one of the principal reasons is the power of the segregationist bloc in Congress. As previously indicated, by endowing private business and local authorities with unprecedented power to determine the racial pattern in housing, and then taking no steps to control the use of this power, the Federal government indirectly gives major support to intensification of racial segregation. It is fair to say that the segregationist group, through its power in Congress, is able to enforce its views upon the whole country.

In lieu of equal access to Federal housing benefits generally, the housing agencies have developed several devices for assisting minorities to obtain housing. Most important of these in the postwar period has been the purchase by the Federal National Mortgage Association of mortgages on new housing intended for minority occupancy. The FNMA has functioned generally as a market for government-insured or guaranteed mortgages which private investors, for various reasons, were unwilling to acquire. For certain types of housing the FNMA engages in essentially direct lending by giving advance commitments to purchase mortgages, thus enabling lenders to originate loans for immediate sale to "Fanny May." Although minority housing has not been explicitly designated as a subject for FNMA assistance, developers of housing tracts for nonwhite occupancy have depended heavily on financing from this source.

Bills have been introduced in Congress, but not passed, to recognize housing for or available to minority groups as one of the categories for FNMA "special assistance," and to provide specific appropriations for the purpose. These proposals have been one aspect of housing policy for minorities on which southern congressmen and northern liberal and labor groups could agree, but significantly they have not attracted the support of the major Negro advancement organizations. The latter, apparently, have preferred not to blur the equal rights issue by supporting housing assistance for particular racial groups.

Another special aid is the Voluntary Home Mortgage Credit Program authorized in the Housing Act of 1954. Its purpose is to obtain FHA or VA loans from private lenders for two categories of disadvantaged borrowers: those residing in small towns or rural areas where mortgage funds are scarce, and members of minority groups wherever situated. Applications from minority home buyers for assistance under this program have been far fewer than expected. Fewer than 5,000 loans were arranged for minority borrowers during the first two and a half years of the program, amounting to less than one-fifth of the total. The comparatively small demand for mortgage assistance by the minority groups is probably owing to several factors. In the first place, studies have shown that credit is generally available to qualified minority home buyers within recognized minority residence areas. Many properties, however, which minority purchasers are able to acquire, do not conform to FHA or VA loan standards because of location or character. There is also evidence that when mortgage assistance was offered through the VHMC Program, it was usually made available at higher discounts than were current in the normal mortgage market. The high cost of such credit to minority buyers may have been one of the factors limiting the demand for assistance through the program.

A third type of special attention to the needs of minority groups is represented in the employment of staffs of Racial Relations Advisors. These officers have the difficult assignment of promoting minority participation in the housing programs without touching the main barriers to that participation. They have worked to obtain as much housing as possible for minority groups, including allocations of public housing units and stimulation of private building for nonwhite occupancy under the FHA program. As housing agencies have become sensitive to the issue of segregation, the Racial Relations Advisors have been allowed to encourage open-occupancy projects both public and private. In this, the racial relations staffs have had to proceed circumspectly because they must not infringe upon the agencies' basic policy of letting local authorities and private builders make the decisions concerning the racial pattern. A too positive advocacy of racial equality has led to bureaucratic trouble for individual officers.

Several other factors have limited the influence of the racial relations staffs. Their duties are wholly advisory with no line administrative or decision-making responsibilities. The positions are considered "Negro jobs," for, with rare exceptions, only Negroes are employed. This practice tends to identify racial matters as being of concern only to Negroes. In urban renewal—the program with greatest direct impact on minority groups—Racial Relations Advisors have not been used beyond a token extent.

Privately Developed Open-occupancy Housing

Although the private building industry is almost solidly committed to racial segregation, there has been a significant slight trend toward racially unrestricted housing developments.[3] Before any legal requirements were in effect for nondiscrimination, a few private builders in various parts of the country and a larger number of housing coöperatives had marketed development housing to an interracial clientele. About fifty genuinely interracial proj-

---

[3] This subject is examined at length in Eunice and George Grier, *Privately Developed Interracial Housing: An Analysis of Experience* (see Appendix).

ects were privately built in the decade following World War II. The near future will undoubtedly see a large increase in the number of these developments because of the statutory prohibition of discrimination in publicly assisted housing in six states and the probable adoption of similar laws in other states.

A legal requirement of nondiscrimination will probably remove many of the obstacles faced by the early developers of open-occupancy housing, who acted on their own initiative and in defiance of the housing industry's fixed practice. The principal difficulty encountered has been not in selling the product but in obtaining good sites for interracial developments. Some projects have had considerable trouble with financing. A decade ago some well-planned and -managed interracial coöperatives failed in their attempts to build interracial housing developments because of FHA objections on principle to both the interracial and the coöperative features. FHA has since shifted to encouraging open-occupancy housing, and several large lending institutions have shown a readiness to finance projects of this type according to usual investment standards. Financing does not now seem to be a major barrier.

Opposition to interracial housing on desirable residential sites has come from property owners, builders, real estate brokers, other local business interests, and, most critically, from local governmental authorities. As a result, builders of interracial housing have frequently been compelled to utilize remote or otherwise less attractive sites for their developments. Interior locations, in turn, have reacted adversely on the builder's competitive position in marketing.

The chief reason given by most builders for excluding minorities is the fear that if they did not do so, they would be unable to sell their houses promptly, if at all. This fear has not been confirmed by the experience of those who have built for an unrestricted market. Sales have been slow in some cases; in others, sufficiently rapid. Variations in the rate of sales or rentals seem to be connected mainly with factors of location and housing value, in about the same way as among all-white developments. One instance of extremely slow sales, disastrous to the builders, involved a project situated in a minority district and intended for sale to minority families. When effective demand from the minority groups turned out to be unexpectedly weak (mainly because of prospects' inability to qualify for mortgage loans), the builder turned in desperation to the white market. Some whites bought, but not enough. The location was a fatal handicap. In general, experience in the marketing of open-occupancy housing indicates that if the location and housing value offered are attractive, a sufficient number of whites will not be deterred from buying by the presence of nonwhites, particularly if the number of the latter is not large.

Whether an interracial development tends to become all non-white seems to depend on its location, price range, and the supply of competing housing available to nonwhites. Low-priced projects near existing minority communities are likely to be more attractive to nonwhites than to whites, and developers may have to employ racial quotas to protect the interracial character of a project. The well-known Concord Park development in suburban Philadelphia was flooded with Negro applicants, apparently because at the time it was built (1954–1955) it represented virtually the only new housing which Negroes could buy in the entire Philadelphia area. Projects distant from established minority neighborhoods, however, and selling in the middle price range or higher have rarely attracted more than modest percentages of nonwhites. In some cases, developers of interracial projects have utilized racial quotas, but in others quota controls have not been found necessary.

Organizations for Equal Rights

Organized groups of citizens concerned with equal rights have played and doubtless will continue to play a central role in the movement toward racial equality of opportunity. It has always been characteristic of American democracy that whenever a public problem arises, citizens organize, independently of government, to advocate solutions.[4] The group discrimination problem is no exception. A large number of organizations have come into existence seeking to lessen group prejudice and discrimination and to

[4] "Americans of all ages, all conditions, and all dispositions constantly form associations. . . . If it is proposed to inculcate some truth or to foster some feeling by the encouragement of a great example, they form a society. . . . Thus the most democratic country on the face of the earth is that in which men have, in our time, carried to the highest perfection the art of pursuing in common the object of their common desires. . . ." Alexis de Tocqueville, *Democracy in America*, Vol. II, Book ii, chap. v (New York: Knopf, 1945), pp. 106–107.

promote equal rights and opportunity. Some of these organizations have been long established; others have formed in recent years. Some are militant; others mild. They have been established under the auspices of churches, labor unions, philanthropic organizations, state and municipal governments, and independently. Some are nation-wide in scope; others are limited to a region, a state, a city, or to a district or neighborhood. Many of these groups are represented in the National Association of Intergroup Relations Officials (NAIRO). Some two dozen organizations interested in housing are affiliated with the National Committee Against Discrimination in Housing.[5]

Only government and law can be directly effective on a large scale in reducing or eliminating discriminatory practices. However, it is in the American tradition that initiative, ideas, and pressure for action should come largely from private citizens who interest themselves in the problem. Moreover, it is universal experience that governmental bodies seldom move on controversial issues without strong sustained pressure from organized citizen groups who play the roles of advocate, goad, and watchdog.

Increasingly, the churches of America are defining racial inequality as a moral problem and urging solutions by application

[5] The list of members indicates the variety of nation-wide organizations actively supporting an open housing market: Amalgamated Clothing Workers of America; American Civil Liberties Union; American Council on Human Rights; American Ethical Union; American Friends Service Committee; American Jewish Committee; American Jewish Congress; American Veterans Committee; Americans for Democratic Action; Anti-Defamation League of B'nai B'rith; Council for Social Action, Congregational Christian Churches; Cooperative League of the USA; Friends Committee on National Legislation; Friendship House; International Ladies' Garment Workers' Union; Jewish Labor Committee; League for Industrial Democracy; Migration Division, Puerto Rican Department of Labor; National Association for the Advancement of Colored People; National Association of Intergroup Relations Officials; National Council of Negro Women; National Council of Churches of Christ, Race Relations Department; National Urban League; Presbyterian Church, USA, Department of Social Education and Action; Race Relations Department, American Missionary Association Division, Board of Home Missions, Congregational Christian Churches; United Auto Workers of America; United Steelworkers of America.

In addition to these national organizations, there are many local groups with similar purposes. For example, the Hyde Park–Kenwood Community Conference (Chicago) and the West End Community Conference (St. Louis) conduct programs aiming to stabilize and improve their respective neighborhoods on an interracial basis. In Natick, Massachusetts, the Committee on Homes for Minority Groups terms itself "a group of citizens who extend a welcome to all people of good character who may wish to live in Natick." This local committee, and others which might be mentioned, not only extends a welcome but works to discover houses for sale to minority groups and to find suitable purchasers.

of Christian and Jewish religious principles. Many public pronouncements to this effect have been made by religious leaders of all major faiths. Programs of education and action have been organized under Protestant, Catholic, and Jewish auspices. Some thirty-five Catholic Interracial Councils are active in cities throughout the country. The Jewish Anti-Defamation League of B'nai B'rith has long been in the forefront of the movement for racial and religious equality. In relation to housing discrimination, a notable example of church policy pointed to action is the open-occupancy covenant proposed to Christians by the Presbyterian Church.

. . . It is the policy and purpose of the Presbyterian Church to work for a nonsegregated society as well as a nonsegregated church. . . . The 168th General Assembly calls upon Christians who are contemplating the sale of property to see as of first importance the need of minority families for equal housing opportunities and adequate housing, and to make their houses available to all qualified purchasers without regard to race. . . . Urges sessions to bring Christians together in covenants of open occupancy which will stem the tendency toward "panic selling" and stabilize their neighborhoods on a nonsegregated basis.[6]

It would be misleading to give an impression that the organized groups dedicated to racial equality are powerful. With few exceptions, they have operated on very limited funds, with heavy reliance on volunteer unpaid services to carry out their programs. Hence, in their capacity to campaign for objectives or to sustain an action program, these organizations can hardly be compared with a great many business, professional, or other interest groups. Nevertheless, they have supplied a major part of the stimulus and leadership to recent advances toward racial equality.[7] Their legislative campaigns have been rewarded by a growing body of statutory law against discrimination in northern and western states and cities. They supplied much of the pressure leading to progressive abandonment of the FHA's one-time discriminatory policies. In litigation, the National Association for the Advancement of Colored People has won a series of notable victories over racist state laws.

Only a few agencies, notably the American Friends Service Com-

[6] Minutes of the 168th General Assembly of the Presbyterian Church in the United States of America, Fifth Series, 1956, Vol. 5, pp. 227–228.
[7] A special survey conducted for the Commission by the National Association of Intergroup Relations Officials describes and evaluates the activities of organizations and professional intergroup relations workers in the field of housing (see Appendix).

mittee, have directly promoted unrestricted housing developments, but these few have been instrumental in realizing about half of the pioneering projects of this type.

Although voluntary agencies have carried through a small number of demonstration housing projects, it seems that, for the most part, their activities must be confined to more limited objectives: to the education of the public, to the support of equal rights legislation and government administrative action, to persuading the housing industry to modify its practices, to helping individual minority families obtain homes in good neighborhoods, to stabilizing mixed neighborhoods, to raising the standards of citizenship in minority groups, to supporting appeals to the courts where constitutional rights have been violated. The commission's recommendations deal with some of these lines of action.

Housing for Minorities: A Substitute for Equality

From one point of view, a logical answer to the scarcity of housing available to minority groups is, "Very well, let us build houses for them." This is the answer which the housing industry has attempted to give, supported with diminishing assurance by the Federal housing authorities. During World War II and subsequently, private builders have produced new, standard quality houses for sale and rent to Negroes and other minorities for the first time in history, excepting a very few earlier philanthropically inspired ventures. In amount, this housing has been probably not more than 1 or 2 percent of the total production of new private housing in the postwar period, but its very existence stands in sharp contrast to the earlier almost total neglect of the housing needs of minority groups. In some cities—Memphis, Atlanta, Houston, Los Angeles, and others—new housing built for Negro occupancy runs into thousands of units. Some of the developments, as in Atlanta and New Orleans, are of high quality.[8]

The segregating influence of minority housing was precipitated into public controversy when the National Association of Home

---

[8] The characteristics of successful and unsuccessful minority housing developments are examined in a special study by William Goldner, using data from a survey by the Mortgage Bankers Association of America. A more extended analysis of house building for minorities, based on interviews with more than a hundred builders is contained in *Residence and Race,* Chapter 11: "The House Building Industry." Southern experience is treated in Nathan Glazer (ed.), *Studies in Housing and Minority Groups,* and in the research reports by Thompson, Lewis, and McEntire; Demerath and Associates; and LaViolette (see Appendix).

Builders in 1954 announced a plan to build 150,000 new dwellings for minority groups, and the president of the association urged builders to coöperate in order to preserve segregation against the onslaughts of the Supreme Court and legislatures. Previously, minority leadership, anxious to obtain better living conditions for its constituents, had largely overlooked the segregation aspect of housing for minorities. But the Home Builders' public definition of its program as a lever for segregation provoked the Negro advancement organizations to condemn it. "We do not want jim-crow dwellings whether they are new or old," resolved the NAACP. Subsequently, housing planned for minority occupancy and proposals to stimulate such construction have tended to be viewed more in a civil rights context than from the standpoint of housing supply. The Home Builders have quietly abandoned their once publicized program. Proposals in Congress for Federal assistance to minority housing have received the support neither of the Negro advancement organizations nor of the Home Builders nor of the Federal Housing Administrator.

Builders of minority housing projects have encountered many discouragements. The same pressures which sustain segregation also operate to limit drastically the builder's choice of locations. Typically, the builder of housing for nonwhites is compelled to choose between an in-lying site in a blighted area and a remote one lacking in facilities and amenities of community life. When a good site can be found, it is likely to be seriously overpriced for middle- to low-income housing. The market for minority housing also has frequently proved disappointing to builders. This may seem strange in view of the acknowledged need of the minority groups for better housing. Need, however, is not effective demand, and demand for housing in general is not the same as demand for a particular collection of houses. Those who are able to pay for new housing, who are in the market at a particular time, and who are interested in a particular development are likely to be only a small fraction of the whole nonwhite population in an area. In addition to these general factors, Negro demand for new housing seems also to be limited by the reluctance of many to move far from existing Negro communities, and to some extent by habituation to a comparatively low level of expenditure for housing.

A third handicap is the reluctance of many mortgage credit

sources to finance minority housing developments. Most builders, in fact, describe this as the principal obstacle. As mentioned above, a large proportion of minority housing projects to date has depended upon government financing through FNMA. The negative attitude of lenders arises partly from an adverse racial judgment of Negroes as credit risks, but also, and perhaps to a greater extent, from the genuine disadvantages of minority housing projects as business ventures.

The obstacles to new housing production for minority occupancy have been less severe in the South than in the North and West, particularly as regards the crucial factor of land. In many southern cities, although not all, the Negro population is less hemmed in and has greater access to open land than in the North. The bulk of new housing for nonwhites has been built in the South, and this is likely to continue to be true. Outside the South, it seems doubtful that private builders will find profitable opportunities for the creation of any great amount of minority housing unless substantially assisted by government.

Opportunity to acquire dwellings of certain types in certain locations is not the same as opportunity to compete in the general housing market. Housing for minorities can never fully satisfy the housing needs of the people for whom it is intended because one of the important needs of every person is freedom to choose among the whole range of alternatives. In much of the South, however, for some years to come, the practical alternatives will probably not be segregated minority housing versus an open market, but segregated housing versus no new housing at all. Facing these actual alternatives, men of good will, by no means proponents of segregation, have supported the building of good housing for minority groups as worth while in itself, even though segregated. Negroes in the South often have struggled hard for the opportunity to have good homes, while leaving aside the segregation issue. Under conditions existing in much of the South, it can be maintained, with reason, that the achievement of good housing tends to advance the status of Negroes, both in their own eyes and in the eyes of others, and is, therefore, a step toward equality.

Chapter 5

THE COMMISSION'S RECOMMENDATIONS

GUIDING PRINCIPLES

Fundamental American Principles

In the United States of America the basic guide to all judgments touching race, color, creed, or national origin must be the fundamental principles of the American social order and form of government. These principles, which are both political and religious, require that all men should be free from arbitrary restraints, all should have equal rights, all should have equal opportunities. They imply that every individual should be judged, rewarded, or penalized according to his personal merits and achievements, and not according to the condition of his birth. Discrimination against people because of their race, ethnic descent, or religion violates these basic principles.

Equality before the law.—No principle of American government is more fundamental than that of equality of all citizens before the law. Properly construed, this principle should mean equal treatment of citizens in all their relations with government, including equal access to and equal rights of participation in all facilities and benefits provided by public authority. Government agencies must, of course, establish appropriate standards and criteria to guide their relations with the people. But there should be no place in any public program for differential treatment of people because of race, color, creed, or ethnic origin.

Conflicts of Rights

It is often asserted that to accord equal treatment to members of minority groups would violate certain rightful freedoms of others, such as freedom to associate with persons of one's choice, freedom to manage or dispose of property, or freedom to conduct one's business, including selection of clients or employees. Also sometimes asserted is a "right to choose one's neighbors."

59

It is apparent that potential conflicts of rights exist, and there-fore some principle must be found for determining which rights are superior. Conflicts of rights are, of course, very common and if they were not, there would be less need for courts of law.

In all public affairs, as suggested above, the superiority of rights to equal treatment is clear on principle. No public officer should have any freedom to make racial, religious, or ethnic distinctions, and no private person has any rightful claim to a racially exclu-sive school, neighborhood, park, hospital, housing project, or other facility which has been provided by government.

In the sphere of private activity, on the other hand, though racial discrimination is morally reprehensible, there remains the question of whether the freedom of individuals to discriminate should be curtailed. Individual liberties are never absolute, but in a free society, abridgements of individual freedom must be justified by persuasive demonstration of a public good to be served. In the American tradition there have been three principal grounds for restricting individual liberty which are applicable to the prob-lem of racial discrimination. These are:

1. Private activities affected with a public interest.

When private activities, because of their nature or scope, affect the welfare of large numbers of people, they cease to be purely private and may justifiably be subjected to control in the public interest. Public utilities are the prime example, but the prin-ciple is applicable widely. Employers have been required, in the public interest, to submit to limitations on their freedom to choose employees; proprietors of establishments serving the general public, such as hotels and restaurants, have been limited in their rights to select clients. In housing, the decisions of an individual property owner concerning the occupancy of a single dwelling may not be thought to involve a substantial public interest. But when private business affects the housing opportunities for thousands or millions of people, it must ac-knowledge a responsibility to the public.

2. Inequality of private power.

Respect for individual liberty as a philosophical principle rests upon an assumption of substantial equality of power among individuals, so that no one individual is in a position to do much damage to others. In American history when marked inequalities of private power have developed they have generated a demand for correction. In housing, the minority individual is confronted not merely with the prejudices of other persons but with the power of organized groups to determine where he shall or shall not live. To limit the power of such organizations would be in no way inconsistent with respect for individual liberty.

3. Restriction of liberty to enhance liberty.

It is a matter of common experience that individual freedom of action must be limited in various ways for the express purpose of preserving and extending freedom itself. Traffic control is an obvious example. If people were free to operate their vehicles on city streets as they saw fit, there would promptly be no freedom of vehicle movement for anyone. More broadly, freedom to live in great cities is dependent upon elaborate systems of regulation.

The application of this familiar principle to relations among people of differing racial or ethnic origins has not been better expressed than by Booker T. Washington's homely observation that "the only way to keep a man in a ditch is to get into the ditch with him." In many ways, as studies for this Commission have shown, the enforcement of limitations on the freedom of minority persons brings restrictions on the freedom and opportunities of others as well. Greater liberty for minorities does not necessarily imply less freedom for others, but more likely would bring an increase of individual freedom generally.

The asserted right "to choose one's neighbors" deserves examination. There are some circumstances in which neighbors actually are chosen, as in private clubs, some small coöperatives, certain religious or fraternal colonies. Choice, to have any meaning, must imply a personal relationship among the chosen, analogous to that of personal friends or house guests. There is, however, no choosing of neighbors in ordinary residential areas where dwellings are offered on the housing market. A person seeking a place to live chooses a neighborhood, but other residents of the area do not normally choose him. A right to choose one's neighbors may be recognized in those circumstances where a process of choosing really occurs, but in the typical situation such a right can neither be affirmed nor denied; it is merely irrelevant.

Segregation: The Basic Inequality

Compulsory residential segregation is the basic inequality that underlies or stimulates other forms of discrimination. The Supreme Court has declared enforced segregation in education "inherently unequal." In the housing field, segregation is even more incompatible with equality. Equal opportunity for housing, therefore, in principle and fact, is identical with freedom of all persons to compete in the general housing market in accordance with their individual preferences and ability to pay.

Prejudice versus Discrimination

Measures for equal opportunity should aim at moderating prejudices as well as reducing discrimination, but the latter should be the focus of direct attention. It is misleading to conceive of discrimination merely as a result and prejudice solely as a cause. The two are actually related in the form of a vicious circle, and each is both cause and effect. Prejudice leads to discrimination, but discrimination generates and sustains prejudice, leading to further discrimination.

Discrimination, as overt behavior, can be brought under direct restraints. Prejudices, being subjective feelings, cannot be touched directly but are affected by the environmental influences upon individuals. A lessening of discrimination, by changing the conditions under which race attitudes are formed, may lead to a lessening of prejudice. In housing, moreover, the most important forms of discrimination are not those directly connected with the prejudices of people, but are represented in the practices of governments and the housing industry.

Education versus Action

Education and action should be regarded not as alternatives but as complementary methods of working for racial equality of opportunity. A concrete change in the situation involving minority groups may be a highly effective form of education. Efforts to induce some specific change, by providing a focus and stimulus for public discussion, may also be a fruitful means of educating a community to the evils of race discrimination. If public consent to a new status for minority groups is to be obtained, obviously the public must be informed and educated concerning the issues and alternatives involved. However, as every teacher knows, precept without example is ineffective teaching. Education merely in the form of bombarding the public with words, without demonstration or example, is unlikely to achieve its purpose.

RECOMMENDATIONS

No single measure can produce a major change in the existing system of racial inequality. Many approaches are needed even if some may seem to overlap. Government, at all levels, bears a primary responsibility because of its constitutional duty to treat all citizens equally and because of its great influence on housing. But there is also much which the housing industry can voluntarily do to support equality. Particularly because the housing industry has become a partner of government in the distribution of government benefits, it has a responsibility greater than that of ordinary private business to deal equally with all American citizens. Private or semipublic organizations, including churches, labor unions, and citizen groups particularly dedicated to equal rights, have a vital role to play as leaders of the movement toward racial equality.

Upon the basis of extensive studies, and guided by the foregoing principles, the Commission offers the following recommendations:

The Federal Government

1. In the Housing Act of 1949, Congress declared the goal of national policy in housing to be "a decent home and a suitable living environment for every American family." A related objective, also declared by Congress, is "the elimination of substandard and blighted areas."

Studies carried out for this Commission demonstrate that realization of these goals of national policy is seriously hampered by racial segregation and discrimination in the distribution of housing facilities and benefits provided under Federal laws. Moreover, the policies of the Federal housing agencies which encourage or permit racial distinctions in the distribution of Federal housing benefits are inconsistent with the Constitution of the United States and the spirit of the housing acts of Congress. In the judgment of this Commission, these official acts of commission and omission which lead to discrimination are the product of archaic practices and attitudes which have no place in today's world.

Although Federal programs provide but a part of the aids and resources utilized in the production of housing, the role of the Federal government looms large in this area of our economy and society. It is generally recognized that Federal resources and leadership are crucial to the success of the national effort to achieve a decent home for every American family. In this Report we call upon state and local governments, voluntary associations of citizens, and the housing industry to take certain definite steps to purge our national life of the evil of housing discrimination. All this cannot proceed with any assurance of success unless the Federal government moves to cure the ills of its own programs by the most expeditious yet sound measures.

Toward this purpose we recommend to the President of the United States that he establish a committee on the elimination of discrimination in Federal housing and urban renewal programs. We suggest that this committee be modeled after the presidential committees previously established to carry out the policies of equal employment opportunity under government contracts and equal treatment and opportunity for all persons in the armed services. Like its predecessors, the committee should be composed of high-ranking Federal officials and private citizens, including representation of the housing industry and the groups affected by discrimination in housing.

This presidential committee should have the duty and authority to examine the rules, procedures, and practices of the Federal housing agencies, and consult with representatives of interested groups and the housing industry with the view of determining the best means of achieving the purpose for which it was created. After study of the problems, the committee should present to the President its recommendations for a complete program and time schedule looking toward the elimination of discrimination in the distribution of Federal housing benefits at the earliest time practicable.

2. We further recommend, pending the adoption of Federal measures adequate to insure the equal access of all citizens to Federal housing benefits, and parallel with such measures when adopted, that Federal housing agencies give, without delay, the fullest support to state and municipal legislation for equal treatment in housing.

3. Because of the vital role of local government in many aspects of housing, it is essential that members of minority groups participate fully in the political processes through which local officials, including members of zoning boards, planning commissions, housing authorities, and the like, are selected. Restrictions on voting rights or other barriers to such participation should be removed. We therefore strongly endorse the action of Congress in 1957 to protect the voting rights of citizens; we urge the President, the U. S. Department of Justice, and the Civil Rights Commission to enforce and implement the Civil Rights Act of 1957 in every possible way.

Federal-Local Programs

Major phases of government-assisted housing are planned and administered by Federal and local governments coöperatively. For these programs we offer the following recommendations:

1. Recognizing that equal opportunity to obtain good housing will be most readily achieved when the supply of housing is adequate for the whole population, we recommend that Federal and local housing and urban renewal authorities intensify their efforts to increase the total housing supply. Special efforts should be made to increase the supply of good quality housing economically accessible to middle- and lower-income groups.

2. Authorities in charge of urban renewal programs should recognize, as a primary responsibility, the opening of adequate housing opportunities for displaced families, most of whom belong to minority groups.

3. Urban renewal programs should place increased emphasis on conservation and rehabilitation projects in areas undergoing racial transition, to maintain good housing standards. Special effort should be made to stabilize these areas on an interracial basis.

4. Urban renewal authorities should actively promote housing

developments on open land with unrestricted occupancy, within the incomes of a substantial number of families in central areas. For this purpose, the use of open and predominantly open-land projects authorized by Congress should be actively encouraged.

5. Authorities in charge of low-rent public housing should vigorously combat the tendency for public housing projects to become low-income and racial "ghettos." To this end, intensified effort should be made to develop projects in scattered locations, away from slums, and of such size and character as will blend into the housing pattern in the site areas. Public housing agencies should seek authority to modify the income limitations on continued eligibility for public housing, so that tenant families would not be compelled to leave because their incomes had risen, but could remain, on payment of a fair rent, if they desired to do so.

State Governments

1. We strongly recommend repeal of all existing laws requiring racial segregation.

2. We recommend that state legislatures follow the example of the several states which have enacted legislation prohibiting discrimination in housing. Such laws should, at the minimum, apply to all housing built or financed by any form of public aid. Experience under the New York City law covering all multiple-unit and development housing should be carefully studied for guidance in the extension of state legislation.

3. Agencies of state governments charged with the enforcement of laws against discrimination should have four types of authority, namely:

   a. Power to act upon complaints of violation; to seek voluntary compliance with the law by means of persuasion and conciliation; and if voluntary methods fail, to issue orders and apply for their enforcement in the courts.

   b. Authority to investigate reported practices of discrimination and initiate compliance proceedings on their own initiative, independent of complaints from aggrieved individuals.

   c. Authority to investigate complaints of discriminatory application of state or local laws relating to land use or housing, and to make public the findings of such investigations.

    d. Authority and adequate funds to conduct programs of research, information, and education to encourage public acceptance of an open housing market.

Local Governments

1. In the absence of state laws, we recommend that municipal legislative bodies adopt laws of the type recommended above to states, so far as their authority permits, and provide for their enforcement.

2. Municipal legislatures should declare, as public policy, that all local laws be administered without discrimination, and provision should be made for investigation of alleged violations.

3. Municipal governments should take leadership in developing programs of information and education to encourage public acceptance of an open housing market, on the model of existing programs in several cities.

The Housing Industry

1. We recommend to builders, mortgage lenders, and real estate brokers that they conform to the principle of a free housing market and study the experience of financially successful interracial housing developments for helpful guidance. This action is not only a matter of social responsibility, but it is in the economic interest of the housing industry to broaden the market for housing and remove impediments to its functioning.

2. Individual builders may consider that to admit any nonwhites to their developments would place them under a competitive disadvantage. Such disadvantage, to the extent that it exists, would be greatly lessened or eliminated if builders in a market area acted in concert to open all housing developments to qualified buyers or tenants without regard to race, ethnic descent, or religion. We recommend, therefore, to national and local associations of the housing industry that they take the lead in effecting a concerted, industry-wide policy to this effect.

3. Mortgage lenders should singly or collectively discontinue the practice of limiting loans to nonwhite borrowers in certain resi-

dential districts. Mortgage credit should be extended to nonwhites in any location on the same terms as to other borrowers.

4. Since The National Association of Real Estate Boards has previously deleted from its Code of Ethics all references to race or nationality, we recommend that real estate boards take the positive step of declaring that realtors should offer listed residential properties to any qualified purchaser or renter without regard to racial or religious distinction unless the principal has in writing directed limitation of a particular transaction to certain groups.

5. We urge trade associations of the housing industry, including real estate boards, mortgage banker associations, and builders' associations, to drop color bars to membership and admit any qualified businessman without distinction of race, color, or creed.

Intergroup Relations Organizations

Progress toward the realization of equal opportunity in housing and other fields depends in large measure upon the stimulus and leadership provided by voluntary associations of citizens. We therefore recommend

> 1. That such associations develop effective programs for promoting equality of opportunity in housing and seek ways of carrying out those programs.

Since studies and experience have demonstrated that efforts to educate the public on the issues of equal rights and opportunity are generally most effective when linked with concrete demonstrations or specific action proposals, we recommend

> 2. That voluntary associations emphasize programs of combined action and community education.

As examples of important and much needed programs of action and education, we recommend to voluntary associations activities of the following types:

> 3. Development and support of programs to increase the supply of housing economically accessible to middle- and lower-income groups.
> 4. Efforts to obtain the enactment of sound Federal, state, and municipal laws protecting equal opportunity for housing; enlistment of the support of candidates for elective offices who favor open housing policies.

5. Where nondiscrimination laws have been enacted, co-operation in promoting public understanding and acceptance of the law; taking the lead in mobilizing community support for effective enforcement.

6. Making representations to public officials concerning such discriminatory administration of land use and housing laws as may exist, reminding the officials of their constitutional duty to treat all citizens equally; directing public attention to instances of discriminatory use of public authority.

7. Assisting minority individuals whose legal rights have been violated in utilizing any legally available remedies; supporting litigation in defense of statutory or constitutional rights.

8. Encouraging and assisting trade associations in the housing industry to take action to overcome discrimination in the housing market.

9. Assisting qualified minority families to obtain homes in good neighborhoods by seeking dwellings that may be available, and soliciting the coöperation of the real estate business in this endeavor.

10. In neighborhoods newly entered or likely to be entered by minority families, counseling with local residents and public authorities to calm any racial tensions, prevent flight of white residents, and promote acceptance of an interracial pattern.

11. Stimulating and assisting the residents of racially changing neighborhoods to organize and act for preserving housing standards including adequate public services and enforcement of housing codes, to prevent such neighborhoods from deteriorating into slums.

12. Persuading community institutions such as churches, labor organizations, political associations, and others to adopt and publicly declare positions of support for equal opportunity in housing.

13. Working with the press, radio, and television to secure the fullest publicity concerning issues of housing and minority groups, publicizing both problems and progress

toward their solution; assisting the communications media to obtain accurate information concerning events and issues in the field.

14. As an essential foundation for all the foregoing activities, collecting and making available facts concerning the housing conditions of minority groups, discriminatory practices and their effects, experience with open-occupancy housing including its effects on the housing market and property values, experience with laws against discrimination, public opinion regarding equal opportunity in housing, the changing economic and social status of minority groups, and other relevant matters.

To carry on the suggested activities effectively requires technical knowledge and skill in such fields as real estate, mortgage financing, public relations, law, social and economic research, and community organization. Therefore,

15. We urge organizations working for racial equality in housing to enlist the support and assistance of persons with the essential technical competence.

Finally, though voluntary associations by nature rest upon the participation of their members, to conduct programs of any magnitude or complexity requires trained staff and funds. We therefore recommend

16. That philanthropic foundations and interested persons give financial support to voluntary agencies, national and local, that have soundly conceived programs of action and demonstrate competence in their execution.

THE COMMISSION ON RACE AND HOUSING

Gordon W. Allport	Clark Kerr
Elliott V. Bell	Philip M. Klutznick
Laird Bell	Henry R. Luce
John J. Cavanaugh, C.S.C.	Stanley Marcus
Henry Dreyfuss	Ward Melville
Peter Grimm	Francis T. P. Plimpton
Campbell C. Johnson	R. Stewart Rauch, Jr.
Charles Keller, Jr.	John H. Wheeler

Earl B. Schwulst, Chairman

Appendix

STUDIES AND RESEARCH MEMORANDA PREPARED FOR THE COMMISSION ON RACE AND HOUSING 1956-1958

Studies Published or in Process of Publication

McEntire, Davis, *Residence and Race: Final and Comprehensive Report to the Commission on Race and Housing* (in press).

A comprehensive study of housing and residence problems involving racial and ethnic minority groups in the United States. It brings together the principal findings of the entire program of research carried on for the Commission on Race and Housing.

The author is Professor of Social Welfare, University of California at Berkeley, and Research Director for the Commission on Race and Housing.

Glazer, Nathan (ed.), *Studies in Housing and Minority Groups.*

A collection of local studies on housing conditions and problems involving racial or ethnic minority groups in nine large cities, with an introduction by the editor. Groups and cities studied include Negroes in Atlanta, Birmingham, Detroit, and New Orleans; Mexican-Americans in Houston and San Antonio; Japanese-Americans in San Francisco; and Puerto Ricans in New York.

Contributing authors include Jack E. Dodson, formerly Assistant Professor of Sociology, University of Texas; Morris Eagle, Research Fellow, Research Center for Mental Health, New York University, and Instructor in Psychology, Finch College, New York; Giles Hubert, Professor of Economics and Business Administration, Dillard University, New Orleans; Harry H. L. Kitano, Acting Assistant Professor in Social Welfare, University of California at Los Angeles; Forrest E. LaViolette, Professor of Sociology, Tulane University, New Orleans; Hylan Lewis, formerly Professor of Sociology, Atlanta University, Atlanta; Albert J. Mayer, Associate Professor of Sociology, Wayne State University, Detroit; Joseph T. Taylor, formerly Professor of Sociology, Dillard University, New Orleans; Robert A. Thompson, Housing Secretary, Atlanta Urban League, Atlanta.

The editor is a member of the faculty of Bennington College, Bennington, Vermont, formerly Associate Editor of *Commentary*, and Lecturer in Sociology at the University of California, Berkeley.

Goldner, William, *New Housing for Negroes: Recent Experience* (published as Research Report No. 12, Real Estate Research Program, University of California, Berkeley, 1958).

An analysis of data gathered by the Mortgage Bankers Association of America in 1955 on new, private housing developments for Negro occupancy in the United States. More than eighty sales or rental developments are examined. Emphasis is on a comparative analysis of characteristics of successful and unsuccessful projects.

Dr. Goldner prepared the report while a member of the Business Administration faculty, Bowling Green State University, Ohio.

Grier, Eunice and George, *Privately Developed Interracial Housing: An Analysis of Experience.*

A study of the experience of some fifty private housing developments open on initial occupancy to members of all races. The auspices, planning, location, financing, marketing, and other aspects of interracial developments are analyzed. Data were gathered through on-site observation and interviews with developers, housing occupants, public officials, and others.

The authors are specialists in human relations research and residents of an interracial community.

Laurenti, Luigi, *Property Values and Race: Studies in Seven Cities.*

An analysis of the effect on property values of nonwhite entry into formerly all-white residential neighborhoods. The study is based on an analysis of some ten thousand property transfers in selected areas of San Francisco and Oakland, California, and Philadelphia, supplemented by data from other studies in Chicago, Detroit, Kansas City, and Portland, Oregon, and by extensive interviews with real estate brokers, property appraisers, and others.

Dr. Laurenti was formerly Assistant Head of Business Administration, University of California Extension, San Francisco, and is now a business corporation executive in California.

Rapkin, Chester, *The Demand for Housing in Racially Mixed Areas: A Philadelphia Study*. Prepared at the Institute for Urban Studies, University of Pennsylvania, with the assistance of William Grigsby, Thomas Shea, Janet Scheff, George Moed, and Hilda Hertz.

An analysis of factors affecting the demand for housing by whites and nonwhites in four racially mixed residential areas of Philadelphia. The study is based on data of property transfers and interviews with home buyers.

The author is Research Associate Professor, Institute for Urban Studies, University of Pennsylvania, and an Economic Consultant in New York City.

Stetler, Henry G., *Racial Integration in Private Residential Neighborhoods in Connecticut*. In coöperation with the State of Connecticut, Commission on Civil Rights, Research Division. Published by the Connecticut Commission on Civil Rights, 1957.

A study of selected, stable neighborhoods in Connecticut cities occupied by both white and Negro families. Data were obtained by interviews with more than 600 residents and relate to the characteristics of Negro and white families in the study neighborhoods, experiences of Negroes in obtaining houses, social relations, and interracial attitudes.

The author is Research Supervisor in the Connecticut Commission on Civil Rights.

Unpublished Reports

Note.—It is anticipated that several of these reports will be published in some form. Those not published will be deposited in the library of the University of California, Berkeley.

Amerman, Helen E., Studies of Attitudes Toward Housing and Race.

A comparative analysis of the findings of approximately twenty-five studies, conducted between 1926 and 1954, on attitudes of people toward racial residential segregation and related questions. Racial attitudes and values associated with housing are further examined as supporting factors for segregation.

The author is Assistant Director of the Council for Civic Unity of San Francisco and was formerly on the research staff of the Commission on Race and Housing.

Case, Fred E., R. Clay Sprowls, and S. Lynn Clark, The Housing Status of Mexican-American Families in Central Los Angeles.

A report of a sample survey of approximately 750 Mexican-American households in Los Angeles. Data are presented on household characteristics, family income, housing conditions, preferences, and house financing arrangements.

Dr. Case and Dr. Sprowls are Associate Professors and Mr. Clark is Research Associate in the School of Business Administration, University of California at Los Angeles.

Case, Fred E., James H. Kirk, and S. Lynn Clark, The Housing Status of Minority Families in Los Angeles. Prepared in coöperation with the Los Angeles Urban League.

A report of a sample survey covering approximately 700 minority families, predominantly Negro, in Los Angeles. Data include household characteristics, financial status, housing conditions and preferences.

Dr. Kirk is Professor of Sociology, Loyola University of Los Angeles. The other authors are identified above.

Clarkson, Diana, Sunnyhills: A Privately Developed Interracial Housing Project.

A case history of an interracial housing development in Santa Clara County, California, sponsored by the American Friends Service Committee and the United Automobile Workers. Data were gathered from personal interviews, minutes of meetings, and records of the American Friends Service Committee.

The author was on the research staff of the Commission on Race and Housing.

Demerath, Nicholas J., and Associates, Private Enterprise Housing for Negroes in Seven Metropolitan Areas.

A survey of house-building and mortgage-financing practices and experience in relation to new housing for sale or rent to Negroes. The report is based chiefly on interviews with some 200 builders, lenders, and brokers in the metropolitan areas of Birmingham, Chicago, Detroit, Los Angeles, Norfolk, St. Louis, and San Francisco.

The author was formerly Professor and Chairman, Organization Research Group, Institute for Research in Social Sciences, University of North Carolina. Associated in the survey were William Goldner, formerly of the Department of Business Administration, Bowling Green State University, Ohio; R. Clay Sprowls, School of Business Administration, University of California at Los Angeles; Floyd K. Hunter, School of Social Work, University of North Carolina; Richard Simpson and Ida H. Simpson, Department of Sociology, Pennsylvania State University.

A special section of the report is an analysis of the power structure of the housing industry prepared by Dr. Hunter from interview material.

Edwards, E. Franklin, and Harry J. Walker, The Impact of Urban Renewal on Minority Group Housing Opportunities in Six Cities.

A field study of urban renewal programs in relation to housing of minority groups in Birmingham, Chicago, New York, Norfolk, Philadelphia, and Washington, D. C. Special attention is given to problems and implications of relocation of population from urban renewal areas.

The authors are members of the faculty of the Department of Sociology, Howard University, Washington, D. C.

Harvey, June E., A Selected Bibliography of Housing and Race.

A selected, classified bibliography of research materials pertaining to housing and minority groups.

The author is Editorial Assistant to the Research Director, Commission on Race and Housing.

Helper, Rose, The Role of the Real Estate Business in Minority Group Housing: A Chicago Study.

An analysis of data gathered in interviews with ninety real estate brokers in three areas of Chicago undergoing racial transition in 1956. A review of real estate broker policy and practice, as described in the literature since 1920, is also included.

Miss Helper collected the interview data and wrote the report in connection with her doctoral dissertation in Sociology at the University of Chicago.

LaViolette, Forrest E., with the assistance of Joseph T. Taylor and Giles Hubert, Negro Housing in the New Orleans Community.

A study of social, economic, and political factors affecting the availability of housing to Negroes in New Orleans. The roles of public housing, city planning, and private enterprise are considered. Comparative case histories of two Negro residential subdivisions are included.

The author is Head of the Department of Sociology, Tulane University. Dr. Taylor was formerly Professor of Sociology at Dillard University, New Orleans. Dr. Hubert is Professor of Economics and Business Administration at Dillard.

Masuoka, Jitsuichi, and Preston Valien, A Memorandum on Social Consequences of Racial Residential Segregation. Prepared in the Department of Social Sciences, Fisk University, Nashville, Tennessee, with the assistance of Donald Ferron, Annie Okleton, and Bonita H. Valien.

An analytical review and summary of research literature pertaining to the social consequences of racial residential segregation, with extensive supporting quotations from published and unpublished sources. Also includes material from a survey among Fisk University students concerning housing values of middle-class Negroes.

The authors are, respectively, Professor of Social Science and Chairman, Department of Social Sciences, Fisk University.

Nason, Milton, Comparative Analysis of White and Nonwhite Home Mortgage Experience Based on Data from the Census of Housing, 1950.

A statistical study of differentials in home mortgage financing according to color of owners, based on the Survey of Residential Financing, Census of Housing, 1950.

The author was formerly on the research staff of the Commission on Race and Housing, and is now a practicing attorney in California.

Nason, Milton, Negro-Owned and Operated Savings and Loan Associations.

A report of a questionnaire survey of Negro-owned and -operated savings and loan associations, 1956. Questionnaire data from nineteen associations were augmented through interviews and correspondence with officials of the United States Savings and Loan League, Department of Commerce, Federal Housing Administration, and the Home Loan Bank Board.

National Association of Intergroup Relations Officials, The Professional Intergroup Relations Worker and Minority Housing Problems.

A report of a mail questionnaire survey of approximately 450 intergroup relations agencies concerning activities in the housing field. Under the auspices of NAIRO, the survey was conducted by Helen E. Amerman. Eunice and George Grier analyzed the data and prepared the report. (To be published by NAIRO.)

Population Research and Training Center, University of Chicago, Illustrative Projections of United States Population by Color, Urban-Rural Residence, and Broad Region to 1975. Prepared under the direction of Philip M. Hauser.

Population projections under alternative assumptions of fertility and level and patterns of migration, with analytical text. The data are summarized in *Residence and Race,* the final report to the Commission on Race and Housing.

Reid, Margaret G., Housing in Relation to Income.

A statistical analysis of white-nonwhite differentials in the relationships of housing and family income, based on special tabulations of 1950 Housing Census data.

Dr. Reid is Professor of Economics at the University of Chicago.

Selltiz, Claire, and Stuart W. Cook, Studies in the Social Psychology of Race and Housing.

1. "How People Feel and Act about Interracial Housing."
2. "Factors Influencing Actions Regarding Interracial Housing."
3. "An Evaluation of the Probable Impact of Various Types of Action to Encourage Interracial Housing."

These three papers were prepared at the Research Center for Human Relations, New York University. The first examines beliefs, attitudes, actions, and motivations of white Americans concerning racially mixed neighborhoods. The second focuses on influences which may affect an individual's behavior toward the development or prevention of interracial neighborhoods. Both sets of considerations are drawn together in the third paper to evaluate possible courses of action for encouraging racial integration in housing. Data are drawn from previous studies, published and unpublished, and from the other research reports prepared for the Commission on Race and Housing.

The authors are respectively Research Associate in the Research Center for Human Relations, and Head, Department of Psychology, Graduate School of Arts and Science, New York University.

Sollen, Robert H., Real Estate Board Policies Toward Minority Groups in a Southern California Urban Community.

A case study centering on the publicized disciplining of two brokers by their real estate board, allegedly for having sold properties in "Anglo" neighborhoods to minority families.

The author is a California newspaperman, formerly Editor of the South Gate *Press*.

Thompson, Robert A., Hylan Lewis, and Davis McEntire, Southern Approaches to Housing for Negroes: A Comparative Study of Atlanta and Birmingham.

A comparative study of housing conditions and opportunities for Negroes in Atlanta, Georgia, and Birmingham, Alabama, respectively reputed to be liberal and conservative southern cities in regard to race relations. Data are drawn from records of the Atlanta Urban League, official documents, newspaper reports, and extensive interviews with white and Negro civic leaders, housing industry representatives, and public officials.

Virrick, Elizabeth L., Negro Housing in Dade County (Florida).

A field study of Negro housing conditions and trends in the county containing Miami, Florida. Emphasis is on new housing construction for Negro occupancy and civic efforts for improvement of housing conditions affecting Negroes.

The author is Hoover Research Fellow at the University of Miami and has long been active in civic affairs in Miami, especially in relation to housing and planning.

www.ingramcontent.com/pod-product-compliance
Lightning Source LLC
Chambersburg PA
CBHW031139270326
41929CB00011B/1685